OLYMPIAD WORKBOOK

01 Learning Objectives

02 Multiple Choice Questions

03 HOTS (Achievers Section)

04 Model Test Paper

05 Answer Keys and Solutions

06 OMR Answer Sheet

V&S PUBLISHERS

Published by:

V&S PUBLISHERS

F-2/16, Ansari road, Daryaganj, New Delhi-110002
☎ 23240026, 23240027 • *Fax:* 011-23240028
✉ info@vspublishers.com • 🌐 www.vspublishers.com

Online Brandstore: amazon.in/vspublishers

Regional Office : Hyderabad
5-1-707/1, Brij Bhawan (Beside Central Bank of India Lane)
Bank Street, Koti, Hyderabad - 500 095
☎ 040-24737290
✉ vspublishershyd@gmail.com

Follow us on:   

BUY OUR BOOKS FROM: AMAZON   FLIPKART

© **Copyright:** *V&S* PUBLISHERS
ISBN 978-81-977325-5-3
New Edition

PUBLISHER'S NOTE

V&S Publishers has carved a significant niche in the publishing industry over the last decade, having successfully published more than 1000 titles across 9 languages spanning over 50 subject categories. Being known for the quality of content, we have built a reputation of excellence and reliability. We have consistently delivered **"Value & Substance"** to our readers, through a wide range of titles across a variety of genres covering school books, fiction and non-fiction that caters to different people from every section of the society.

The **Olympiad Guidebooks for classes 1-10** across all subjects, launched almost a decade ago, under the **GEN X Imprint**, became a go-to-source for the school students in no time, owing to their invaluable and substantive content written in a guidebook pattern,.

Having successfully sold a million copies of the same and in response to demand by both students as well as shopkeepers nationwide; we now present before you our newly launched **Olympiad Workbook Series**, designed for **classes 1-10 across 4 subjects**.

The workbooks are meticulously curated by a team of experienced educators, researchers and subject matter experts, edited by professionals and peer reviewed by teachers. The team has poured its efforts and expertise into creating a crisp and concise workbook which will help and guide the students to the path of success in Olympiad exams. The **MCQs** identified will not only help in scoring top marks in Olympiads but also inculcate a sense of deeper understanding of the subject, by way of solving **HOTS** and referring to complete solutions at the end of the book.

Here we present our new release– **OLYMPIAD WORKBOOK (IMO) CLASS–6** having following features:

- ☞ Based on the latest syllabi
- ☞ MCQs with comprehensive coverage of topics
- ☞ HOTS Questions liberally included
- ☞ A dedicated chapter on logical reasoning
- ☞ Model test paper for thorough practice
- ☞ Sample OMR sheet for real time simulation

We have made sure through our best efforts, that this workbook strictly follows the latest syllabi and patterns of the Olympiad Examination.

As **V&S Publishers** continuously strive to enhance the readability and maintain the credibility of our academic publications, we seek the support of our valuable readers in influencing and enriching the lives of future generations of students.

P.S. While every care has been taken to ensure the correctness of the content, if you come across any error, howsoever minor, do not hesitate to discuss with teachers while pointing that out to us in no uncertain terms.

We wish you all the best for your exams!

DISTINCTIVE FEATURES

01

Learning Objectives

They list the whole chapter as subtopics, helping the teachers to guide children in a step-by-step manner.

02

Multiple Choice Questions

MCQs act as an excellent learning aid, helping you to understand and work on your mistakes.

03

HOTS (Achievers Section)

The High Order Thinking Questions aim to help the student to solve Application-based questions and gain practical understanding of the subject.

Model Test Paper

Model test paper are provided at the end of each book, which help the student to test the knowledge which they have gained after thorough reading of all chapters.

04

Answer Key

Detailed Answer Key along with explanations aid the pupil to indentify, understand the mistakes they make during the course of Olympiad preparation.

05

CONTENTS

NUMBER SYSTEM

LEARNING OBJECTIVES

➤ System of writing numbers
➤ Face value and Place value of numbers
➤ Roman Numerals

MULTIPLE CHOICE QUESTIONS

1. What is the round off value of the product of 43 and 78 ?
   (A) 2800 (B) 3200
   (C) 3500 (D) 3510

2. What number must be subtracted from 1101010 to get 336414 ?
   (A) 754696 (B) 765496
   (C) 764569 (D) 764596

3. The population of a town in the year 2010 was 14693675. In the following year, the population became 18002403. What is the increase in the population?
   (A) 3308728 (B) 3327827
   (C) 3306728 (D) 3206728

4. In the given numbers which will exactly come in the middle in terms of its value?
   3307, 3279, 3467, 3502, 3379, 3667, 3287
   (A) 3307 (B) 3379
   (C) 3467 (D) 3287

5. For making 16 shirts 44 metres of cloth is needed. How much cloth is required for 4 shirts?
   (A) 10m (B) 11m
   (C) 12m (D) 13m

6. A rope of length 20m has been divided into 8 pieces of the same length. What is the length of each piece?
   (A) 1.25m (B) 2.25m
   (C) 2.50m (D) 2.75m

7. By how much is 5943679 smaller than one crore?
   (A) 4056321 (B) 4146321
   (C) 4066321 (D) 4056221

8. Mr. Sharma saves ₹ 8719 every month. How much money will he save in 12 years?
   (A) ₹ 1255636 (B) ₹ 1255036
   (C) ₹ 1255536 (D) ₹ 1255736

9. A motorcycle costs ₹ 49735. How much will 487 motorcycles cost?
   (A) ₹ 24222945 (B) ₹ 24221945
   (C) ₹ 24210945 (D) ₹ 24220945

10. If 18 flats cost ₹ 68251500, what is the cost of each flat?
    (A) ₹ 3791750 (B) ₹ 3797250
    (C) ₹ 3791250 (D) ₹ 3791500

11. What is the difference between the number 768 and that obtained on reversing its digits?
    (A) 97 (B) 98
    (C) 99 (D) 109

12. What is the sum of the number 387 and the number obtained by reversing the digit of the given number?
    (A) 1160
    (B) 1170
    (C) 1070
    (D) 1150

13. What is the Roman numeral for 92 ?
    (A) XCII
    (B) CXII
    (C) LXXXXII
    (D) LXIV

14. Which of the following is an invalid number?
    (A) XXXX
    (B) XCIX
    (C) XLVI
    (D) CCCXL

15. What is the Hindu – Arabic numeral for CDXLVI ?
    (A) 442
    (B) 446
    (C) 448
    (D) 456

16. What is the difference of place value and face value of 7 in the number 30972 ?
    (A) 63
    (B) 65
    (C) 965
    (D) 963

17. A car covers 570 km in 16 hours. What is the speed of the car?
    (A) 35.625 km/h
    (B) 35.325 km/h
    (C) 35.425 km/h
    (D) 35.525 km/h

18. Which of the following is meaningful?
    (A) XXXX
    (B) XVV
    (C) IC
    (D) XCI

19. A factory produces 6097 screws per day. How many screws will it produce in the month of September 2015 ?
    (A) 182941
    (B) 182910
    (C) 189007
    (D) None of these

20. By how much is 7346879 smaller than one crore?
    (A) 2653151
    (B) 2653141
    (C) 2653131
    (D) 2653121

21. The mass of each gas cylinder is 14kg 250-g. What is the total mass of 19 such cylinders?
    (A) 270.25kg
    (B) 272.75kg
    (C) 270.75kg
    (D) None of these

22. The difference between two numbers is 9470587. If the smaller number is 6976583, what is the greater number?
    (A) 16457170
    (B) 16447170
    (C) 16447071
    (D) 16437170

23. Which of the following is correct?
    (A) 29047 > 29153 > 28956
    (B) 28043 > 27654 > 26098
    (C) 30067 > 29804 > 29987
    (D) 40167 > 42157 > 42117

24. A number exceeds 3760924 by 39067. What is that number?
    (A) 3799871
    (B) 3799891
    (C) 3799991
    (D) None of these

25. The cost of a chair is ₹ 1479. How much will 479 chairs cost?
    (A) ₹ 706441
    (B) ₹ 708441
    (C) ₹ 707441
    (D) None of these

HOTS (ACHIEVERS SECTION)

26. A car moves at a uniform speed of 65 km per hour. How much distance will it cover in 25 hours?
    (A) 1525 km
    (B) 1625 km
    (C) 1675 km
    (D) 1645 km

27. What is the product of sum and difference of largest 3-digit number and smallest 3-digit number?
    (A) 988001
    (B) 98801
    (C) 988011
    (D) None of these

28. A factory produces electric bulbs and 2 out of every 10 bulbs is defective. The factory produces 820 bulbs per day. What are the number of defective bulbs produced each day?

(A) 82   (B) 84

(C) 164   (D) 168

29. The diameter of a wheel of a car is 70 cm. How many revolutions will it make to travel 1.65 km?

(A) 650

(B) 750

(C) 800

(D) 850

30. If 15 tins of same size contains 234 kg of oil, how much oil will there be in 20 such tins?

(A) 292 kg

(B) 302 kg

(C) 312 kg

(D) 322 kg

1.	Ⓐ Ⓑ Ⓒ Ⓓ	7.	Ⓐ Ⓑ Ⓒ Ⓓ	13.	Ⓐ Ⓑ Ⓒ Ⓓ	19	Ⓐ Ⓑ Ⓒ Ⓓ	25.	Ⓐ Ⓑ Ⓒ Ⓓ
2.	Ⓐ Ⓑ Ⓒ Ⓓ	8.	Ⓐ Ⓑ Ⓒ Ⓓ	14.	Ⓐ Ⓑ Ⓒ Ⓓ	20.	Ⓐ Ⓑ Ⓒ Ⓓ	26.	Ⓐ Ⓑ Ⓒ Ⓓ
3.	Ⓐ Ⓑ Ⓒ Ⓓ	9.	Ⓐ Ⓑ Ⓒ Ⓓ	15.	Ⓐ Ⓑ Ⓒ Ⓓ	21.	Ⓐ Ⓑ Ⓒ Ⓓ	27.	Ⓐ Ⓑ Ⓒ Ⓓ
4.	Ⓐ Ⓑ Ⓒ Ⓓ	10.	Ⓐ Ⓑ Ⓒ Ⓓ	16.	Ⓐ Ⓑ Ⓒ Ⓓ	22.	Ⓐ Ⓑ Ⓒ Ⓓ	28.	Ⓐ Ⓑ Ⓒ Ⓓ
5.	Ⓐ Ⓑ Ⓒ Ⓓ	11.	Ⓐ Ⓑ Ⓒ Ⓓ	17.	Ⓐ Ⓑ Ⓒ Ⓓ	23.	Ⓐ Ⓑ Ⓒ Ⓓ	29.	Ⓐ Ⓑ Ⓒ Ⓓ
6.	Ⓐ Ⓑ Ⓒ Ⓓ	12.	Ⓐ Ⓑ Ⓒ Ⓓ	18.	Ⓐ Ⓑ Ⓒ Ⓓ	24.	Ⓐ Ⓑ Ⓒ Ⓓ	30.	Ⓐ Ⓑ Ⓒ Ⓓ

PLAYING WITH NUMBERS

LEARNING OBJECTIVES

➤ Types of Number
➤ Divisibility
➤ Multiple and Factors

MULTIPLE CHOICE QUESTIONS

1. Find the largest number that will divide 76, 113 and 186 leaving remainder 4, 5, 6 respectively.
   (A) 24   (B) 12
   (C) 36   (D) 54

2. Find the smallest number which when divided by 16, 36 & 40 leaves a remainder 7 in each case.
   (A) 627   (B) 727
   (C) 827   (D) 927

3. Which greatest number of 4 digits is exactly divisible by 12, 16, 28 & 36?
   (A) 6072   (B) 8072
   (C) 8972   (D) 9072

4. The HCF of two numbers is 23 and their LCM is 1449. If one of the numbers is 161 what is the other?
   (A) 107   (B) 117
   (C) 167   (D) 207

5. Find the smallest number which leaves a remainder 3 when divided by 21, 28, 36 and 45?
   (A) 1163   (B) 1263
   (C) 1283   (D) 1293

6. The HCF of two numbers is 145 and their LCM is 2175. If one of the numbers is 725. What is the other number?
   (A) 5   (B) 290
   (C) 115   (D) 435

7. Which of the following is a composite number?
   (A) 23   (B) 29
   (C) 32   (D) 41

8. Which longest tape can be used to measure exactly the length 7m, 3m 85cm and 12m 95 cm?
   (A) 45 cm   (B) 35 cm
   (C) 105 cm   (D) 70 cm

9. The greatest number that will divide 445, 572 and 699 leaving remainder 4, 5, 6 respectively is
   (A) 84   (B) 42
   (C) 49   (D) 63

10. What is the sum of LCM and HCF of 1152 and 1664?
    (A) 14976   (B) 15104
    (C) 15114   (D) 15204

11. The HCF of two numbers is 21 and their LCM is 3003. If one of the numbers is 231 then what is the other number?
    (A) 273   (B) 263
    (C) 283   (D) 293

12. Find the greatest 3-digit number which is divisible by 8, 10 and 12.
   (A) 840
   (B) 480
   (C) 960
   (D) 980

13. Which of the following number is not divisible by 9?
   (A) 387459
   (B) 904806
   (C) 758934
   (D) 879134

14. Find the smallest possible number which on adding 19 becomes exactly divisible by 28, 36 and 45.
   (A) 1239
   (B) 1241
   (C) 1243
   (D) 1245

15. Four bells toll at intervals 4, 7, 12 and 84 seconds. The bells toll together at 7 o'clock. How many times will they again toll together in 28 minutes?
   (A) 15
   (B) 20
   (C) 25
   (D) 30

16. What is the least 5-digit number which is exactly divisible by 20, 25, 30?
   (A) 10100
   (B) 10200
   (C) 10300
   (D) 10400

17. What is the maximum even multiple of 25 between 500 and 700?
   (A) 660
   (B) 600
   (C) 675
   (D) 650

18. Which of the following number is divisible by 8?
   (A) 162537
   (B) 764918
   (C) 825908
   (D) 694728

19. Which of the following is divisible by 11?
   (A) 65483
   (B) 72493
   (C) 84527
   (D) 92056

20. What is the sum of first five multiples of 23?
   (A) 341
   (B) 342
   (C) 343
   (D) 345

21. Which of the following statement is true?
   (A) 1509344 is divisible by 8.
   (B) 72493 is divisible by 11.
   (C) 8569 is not divisible by 11.
   (D) 115 is a multiple of 19.

22. In 467 * 381 replace * by which smallest digit to make it divisible by 3?
   (A) 1
   (B) 2
   (C) 3
   (D) 4

23. 1870 is divisible by 22. Which two numbers nearest to 1870 are each divisible by 22?
   (A) 1848, 1892
   (B) 1893, 1914
   (C) 1826, 1914
   (D) None of these

24. There are three heaps of rice weighing 120 kg, 144 kg and 204 kg. What is the maximum capacity of a bag so that the rice of each can be packed in exact number of bags?
   (A) 24 kg
   (B) 18 kg
   (C) 12 kg
   (D) 6 kg

25. Four bells ring at intervals of 6, 8, 12 and 20 minutes. They ring simultaneously at 7 a.m. At what time will they ring together next?
   (A) 8 a.m.
   (B) 9 a.m.
   (C) 10 a.m.
   (D) 9:30 a.m.

26. What is the smallest number which when diminished by 7 is divisible by 21, 28, 36 & 45?
    (A) 1260   (B) 1263
    (C) 1267   (D) 1253

27. What is the sum of first five prime numbers which are greater than 100?
    (A) 531   (B) 528
    (C) 529   (D) 533

28. What is the greatest number which divides 285 and 1249 leaving remainder 9 and 7 respectively?
    (A) 134   (B) 136
    (C) 138   (D) 142

29. What is the least number which is divisible by 2, 3, 7, 12, 16, 18 and 30?
    (A) 3040   (B) 4050
    (C) 5040   (D) 5120

30. If 5 is subtracted from three times a number the result is 16. What is the number?
    (A) 7   (B) 8
    (C) 9   (D) 11

Darken Your Choice with HB Pencil

1.	Ⓐ Ⓑ Ⓒ Ⓓ	7.	Ⓐ Ⓑ Ⓒ Ⓓ	13.	Ⓐ Ⓑ Ⓒ Ⓓ	19	Ⓐ Ⓑ Ⓒ Ⓓ	25.	Ⓐ Ⓑ Ⓒ Ⓓ
2.	Ⓐ Ⓑ Ⓒ Ⓓ	8.	Ⓐ Ⓑ Ⓒ Ⓓ	14.	Ⓐ Ⓑ Ⓒ Ⓓ	20.	Ⓐ Ⓑ Ⓒ Ⓓ	26.	Ⓐ Ⓑ Ⓒ Ⓓ
3.	Ⓐ Ⓑ Ⓒ Ⓓ	9.	Ⓐ Ⓑ Ⓒ Ⓓ	15.	Ⓐ Ⓑ Ⓒ Ⓓ	21.	Ⓐ Ⓑ Ⓒ Ⓓ	27.	Ⓐ Ⓑ Ⓒ Ⓓ
4.	Ⓐ Ⓑ Ⓒ Ⓓ	10.	Ⓐ Ⓑ Ⓒ Ⓓ	16.	Ⓐ Ⓑ Ⓒ Ⓓ	22.	Ⓐ Ⓑ Ⓒ Ⓓ	28.	Ⓐ Ⓑ Ⓒ Ⓓ
5.	Ⓐ Ⓑ Ⓒ Ⓓ	11.	Ⓐ Ⓑ Ⓒ Ⓓ	17.	Ⓐ Ⓑ Ⓒ Ⓓ	23.	Ⓐ Ⓑ Ⓒ Ⓓ	29.	Ⓐ Ⓑ Ⓒ Ⓓ
6.	Ⓐ Ⓑ Ⓒ Ⓓ	12.	Ⓐ Ⓑ Ⓒ Ⓓ	18.	Ⓐ Ⓑ Ⓒ Ⓓ	24.	Ⓐ Ⓑ Ⓒ Ⓓ	30.	Ⓐ Ⓑ Ⓒ Ⓓ

BASIC GEOMETRICAL IDEAS 3

LEARNING OBJECTIVES

➤ Polygons
➤ Triangles
➤ Quadrilaterals
➤ Circles

MULTIPLE CHOICE QUESTIONS

1. How many diagonals does a hexagon have ?
(A) 9 (B) 8
(C) 2 (D) 6

2. The pair of adjacent sides in the given quadrilateral is _________.

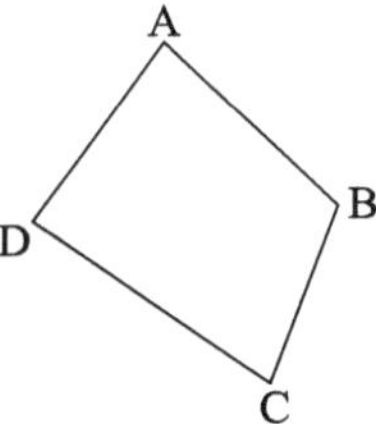

(A) AB, BC (B) AB, CD
(C) BC, AD (D) None of these

3. The center of the circle lies
(A) in the interior of the circle
(B) in the exterior of the circle
(C) on the circle
(D) None of these

4. Which of the given figures is a quadrilateral?

(A) 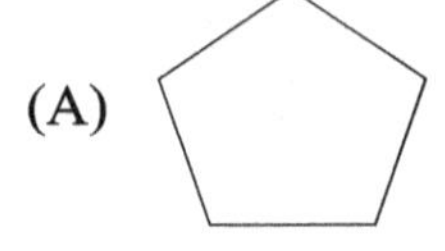 (B) 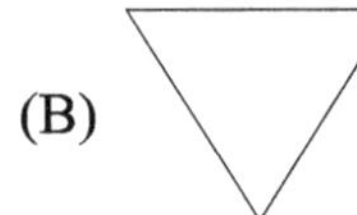

(C) 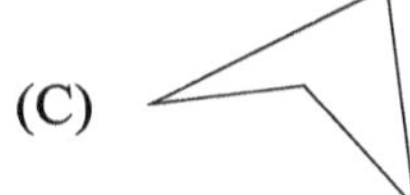 (D) None of these

5. In the given figure, r represents.

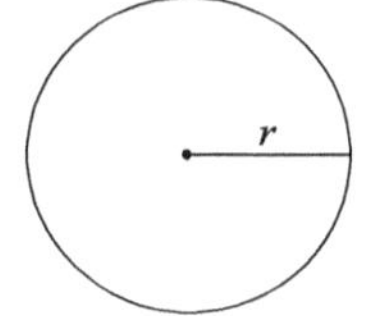

(A) Radius (B) Diameter
(C) Tangent (D) Chord

6. Which two triangles have $\angle B$ as common?

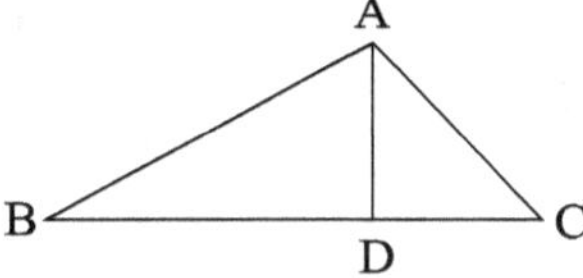

(A) $\triangle ABD$ and $\triangle ADC$
(B) $\triangle ABD$ and $\triangle ABC$
(C) $\triangle ABC$ and $\triangle ADC$
(D) None of these

7. In the adjoining figure, 18 in is the length of

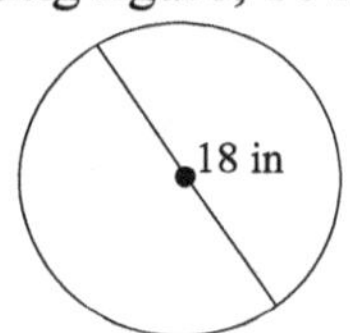

(A) Radius
(B) Diameter
(C) Any chord other than the diameter
(D) None of these

8. The shaded portion of the circle represents.

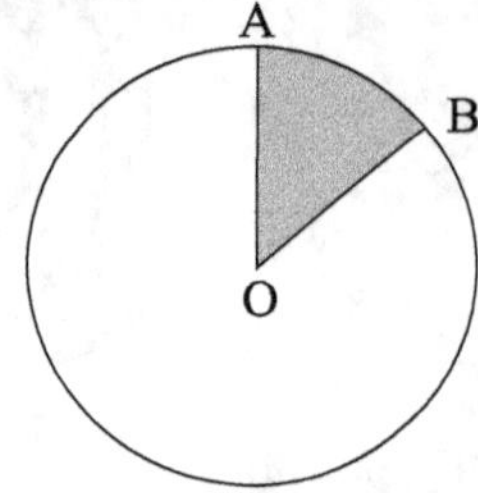

(A) Semicircle
(B) Diameter
(C) A sector of the circle
(D) Segment

9. A chord divides a circle into two
(A) Diameter   (B) Semicircle
(C) Sectors   (D) Segments

10. The centres of a set of circle,each of radius 3, lies on the circle $x^2 + y^2 = 25$. The locus of anypoint in the set is
(A) $4 \leq x^2 + y^2 \leq 64$ (B) $x^2 + y^2 \leq 25$
(C) $x^2 + y^2 \geq 25$ (D) $3 \leq x^2 + y^2 \leq 9$

11. Plane figure with three sides is called
(A) rectangle   (B) triangle
(C) quadrilateral   (D) none of these

12. Plane figure with five sides is known as
(A) octagon   (B) hexagon
(C) pentagon   (D) none of these

13. Where does the vertex of an angle lie?
(A) In its interior   (B) In its exterior
(C) On the angle   (D) None of these

14. The number of angles in figure is

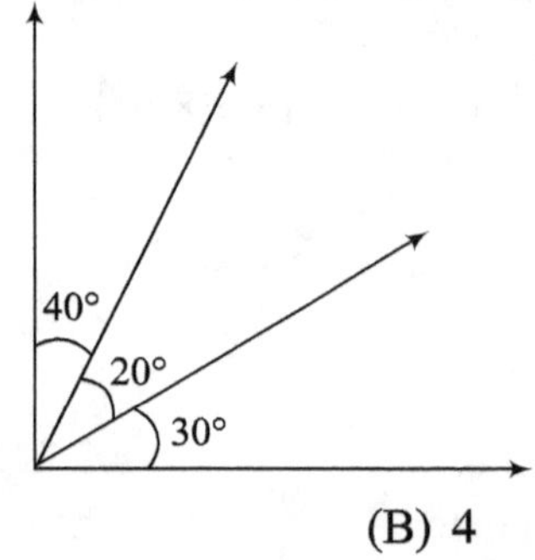

(A) 3   (B) 4
(C) 5   (D) 6

15. In figure, $\angle XYZ$ cannot be written as

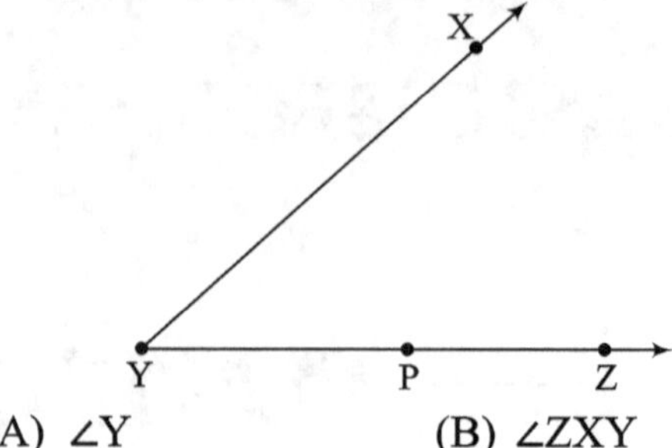

(A) $\angle Y$ (B) $\angle ZXY$
(C) $\angle ZYX$ (D) $\angle XYP$

16. Number of line segments in figure is

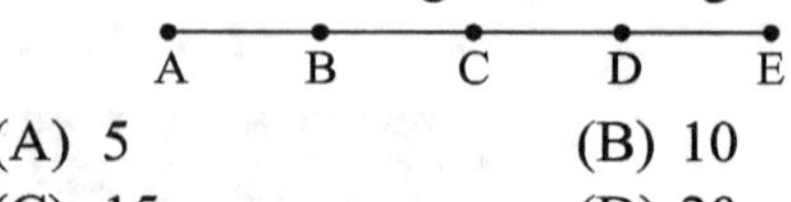

(A) 5   (B) 10
(C) 15   (D) 20

17. A polygon has a prime number of sides. Its number of sides is equal to the sum of the two least consecutive primes. The number of diagonals of the polygon is
(A) 4   (B) 5
(C) 7   (D) 10

18. The number of diagonals in a spetagon is
(A) 21   (B) 42
(C) 7   (D) 14

19. The closed curve which is also a polygon is

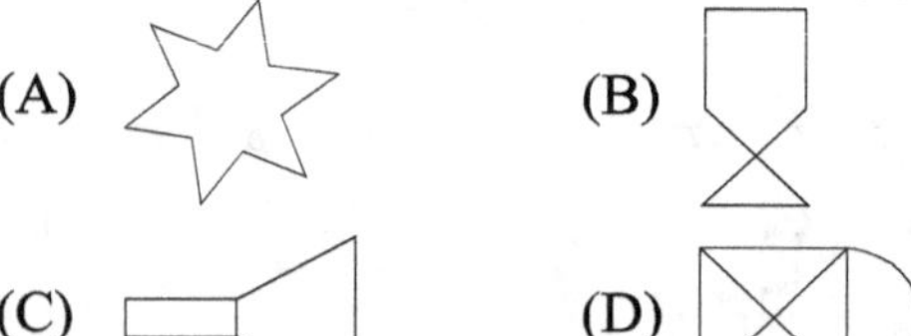

20. In Fig. which of the following is a regular polygon?

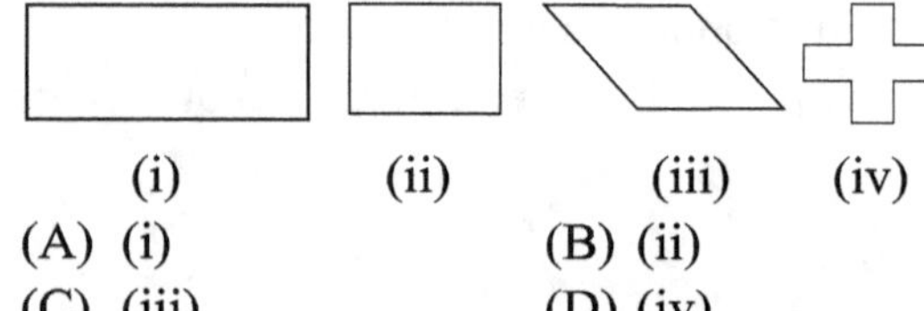

(i)   (ii)   (iii)   (iv)

(A) (i)   (B) (ii)
(C) (iii)   (D) (iv)

21. Which of the following are open curves?

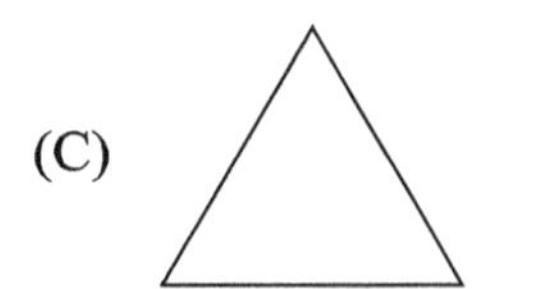 (A) 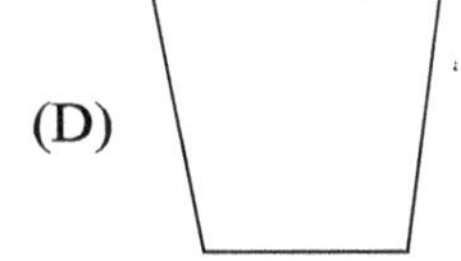 (B)

(C) (D) 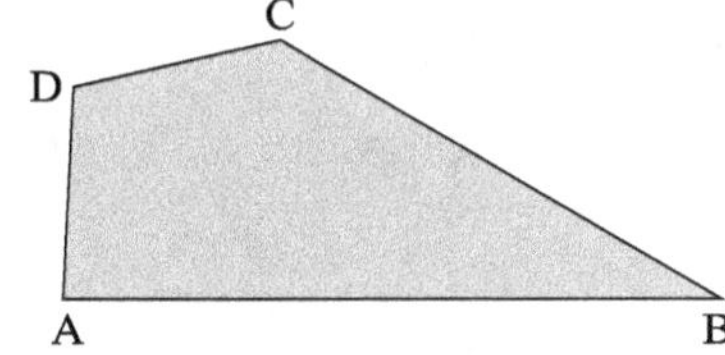

22. Name the angles in the given figure.

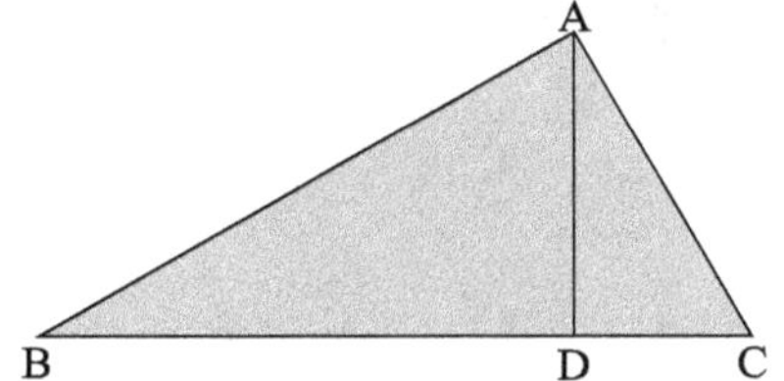

(A) ∠DAB, ∠ABC, ∠BCD and ∠CDA
(B) ∠DBA, ∠ABC, ∠BDC and ∠CDA
(C) ∠DAB, ∠CAB, ∠BCD and ∠CAD
(D) None of these

23. Which two triangles have ∠B as common?

(A) ∠ACD and ∠ADB
(B) ∠ABD and ∠ABC
(C) ∠BAD and ∠BAC
(D) None of these

24. Which of the following statements are true or false:

(i) Two diameters of a circle will necessarily intersect.

(ii) The centre of a circle is always in its interior.

(A) (i) and (ii) are false
(B) (i) and (ii) are true
(C) (i) is true and (ii) is false
(D) (i) is false and (ii) is true

25. Which of the following statement(s) is/are false with respect to quadrilateral?

(A) Each diagonal of a quadrilateral divides it into two triangles.

(B) Each side of a quadrilateral is less than the sum of the remaining three sides.

(C) A quadrilateral can at-most have three obtuse angles.

(D) A quadrilateral has four diagonals.

Darken Your Choice with HB Pencil

1.	Ⓐ Ⓑ Ⓒ Ⓓ	6.	Ⓐ Ⓑ Ⓒ Ⓓ	11.	Ⓐ Ⓑ Ⓒ Ⓓ	16	Ⓐ Ⓑ Ⓒ Ⓓ	21.	Ⓐ Ⓑ Ⓒ Ⓓ
2.	Ⓐ Ⓑ Ⓒ Ⓓ	7.	Ⓐ Ⓑ Ⓒ Ⓓ	12.	Ⓐ Ⓑ Ⓒ Ⓓ	17.	Ⓐ Ⓑ Ⓒ Ⓓ	22.	Ⓐ Ⓑ Ⓒ Ⓓ
3.	Ⓐ Ⓑ Ⓒ Ⓓ	8.	Ⓐ Ⓑ Ⓒ Ⓓ	13.	Ⓐ Ⓑ Ⓒ Ⓓ	18.	Ⓐ Ⓑ Ⓒ Ⓓ	23.	Ⓐ Ⓑ Ⓒ Ⓓ
4.	Ⓐ Ⓑ Ⓒ Ⓓ	9.	Ⓐ Ⓑ Ⓒ Ⓓ	14.	Ⓐ Ⓑ Ⓒ Ⓓ	19.	Ⓐ Ⓑ Ⓒ Ⓓ	24.	Ⓐ Ⓑ Ⓒ Ⓓ
5.	Ⓐ Ⓑ Ⓒ Ⓓ	10.	Ⓐ Ⓑ Ⓒ Ⓓ	15.	Ⓐ Ⓑ Ⓒ Ⓓ	20.	Ⓐ Ⓑ Ⓒ Ⓓ	25.	Ⓐ Ⓑ Ⓒ Ⓓ

UNDERSTANDING ELEMENTARY SHAPES

LEARNING OBJECTIVES

- Measuring of line segments
- Angles and its types
- Triangles and their classifications
- Polygons, quadrilaterals, and solid shapes

MULTIPLE CHOICE QUESTIONS

1. In which of the given figures, the distance between trees is greater.

   (A) A
   (B) B
   (C) Can't be determined
   (D) None of these

2. In given figure, R is near to ___________.

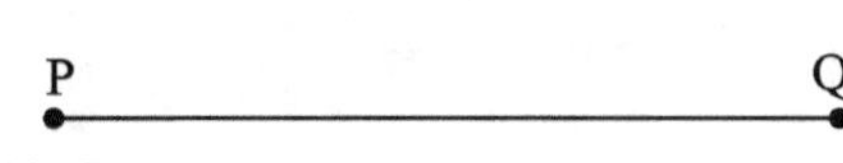

   (A) P
   (B) Q
   (C) Can't say anything
   (D) None of these

3. The length of AB is ________ given in figure.

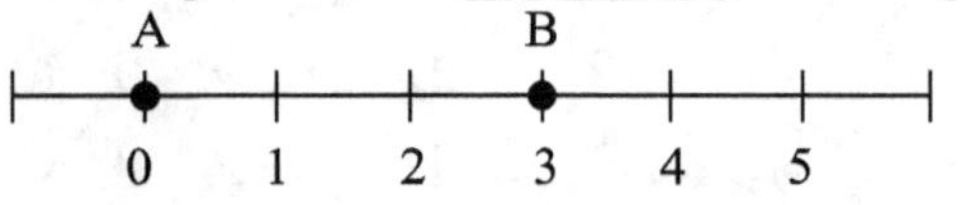

   (A) 3 units   (B) 4 units
   (C) 5 units   (D) 6 units

4. Which of the following is a right angled triangle?

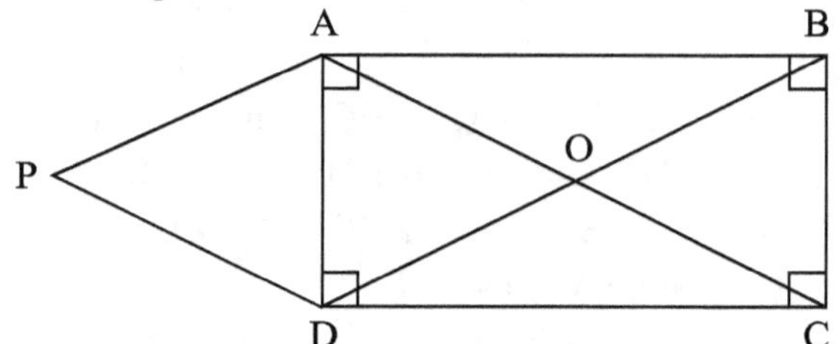

   (A) Δ APD
   (B) Δ DOC
   (C) Δ BDC
   (D) Δ AOD

5. How many faces does the solid in the given figure have?

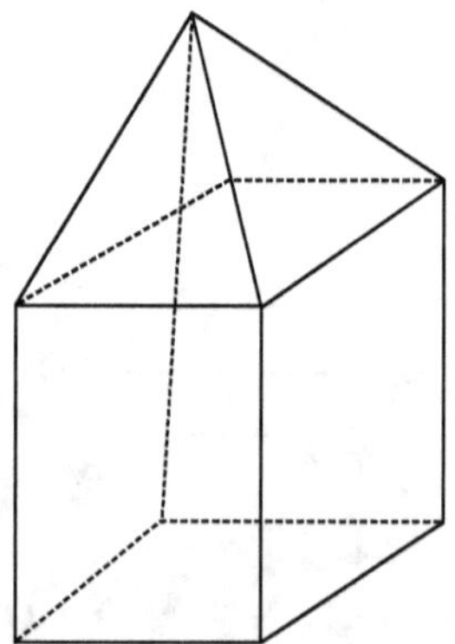

   (A) 5   (B) 7
   (C) 8   (D) 9

6. Which of the following figures has six faces ?

(A) 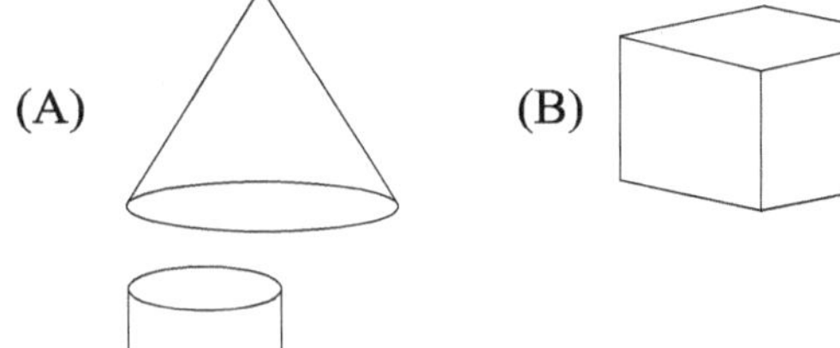 (B)

(C) 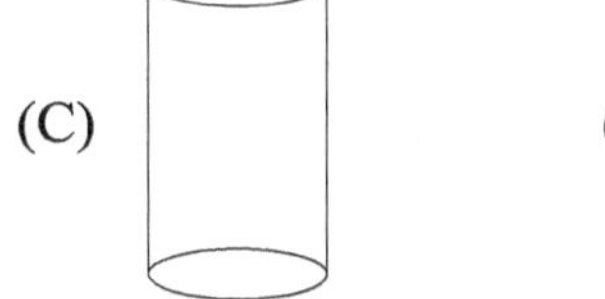 (D)

7. A quadrilateral that is not a parallelogram but has exactly two equal opposite angles is:
   (A) a rhombus   (B) a trapezium
   (C) a square   (D) a kite

8. A triangle with one right angle and two acute angles is called _______ angled triangle.
   (A) Right   (B) Acute
   (C) Obtuse   (D) Scalene

9. AB is a line segment and l is its perpendicular bisector. If P is a point on the line l, then which of the following statements is most satisfying?
   (A) P divides the base AB in the ratio 2 : 3
   (B) P is the centroid Δ PAB
   (C) P is equidistant from A and B
   (D) PA + PB < AB

10. Two position of a block are given below. When 1 is at the top, which number will be at the bottom?

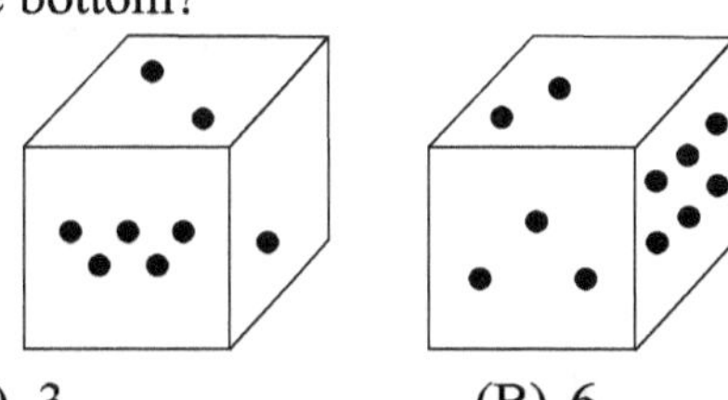

   (A) 3   (B) 6
   (C) 2   (D) 1

11. How many faces does a die have?
   (A) 8   (B) 5
   (C) 6   (D) 4

12. The pair of adjacent sides in the given quadrilateral is _______.

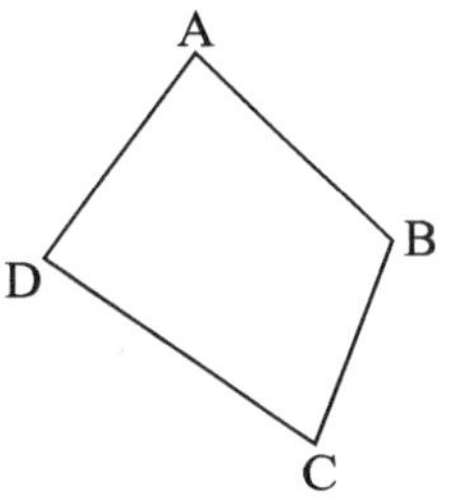

   (A) AB, BC   (B) AB, CD
   (C) BC, AD   (D) None of these

13. Which of the given figures is a quadrilateral?

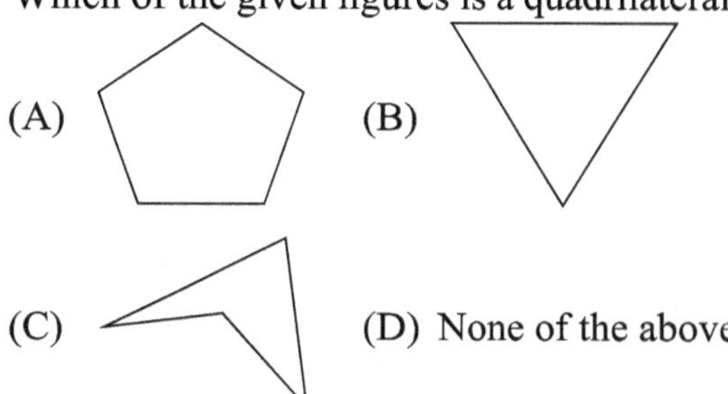

   (A)   (B)

   (C)   (D) None of the above

14. In figure, the reflex ∠AOB is equal to :

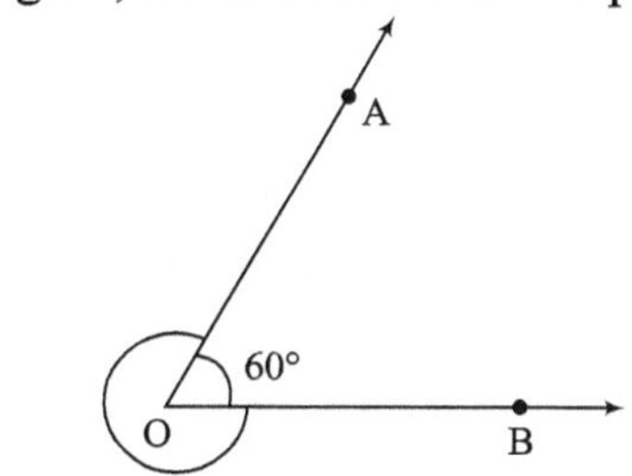

   (A) 60°   (B) 120°
   (C) 300°   (D) 360°

15. Observe the given figure and hence answer the following question.

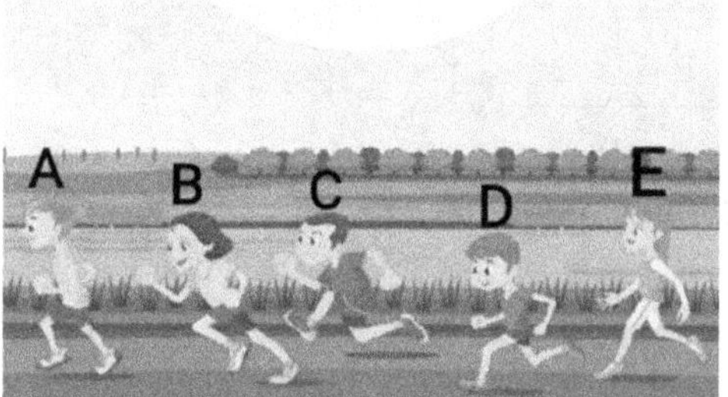

   Which of the two students have larger gap between them?
   (A) A and D   (B) B and E
   (C) D and E   (D) A and E

16. Which of the following method do you prefer to tell that which ball is near to tree in given diagram?

(A) Comparing by observation
(B) Comparing by tracing
(C) Comparison using ruler and divider
(D) Cant be determined.

17. Draw a line segment of PQ of length 15 units and mark a point S on it so that SQ = 5 units, then PS = ________.

(A) 08   (B) 09
(C) 10   (D) 11

18. Draw a line segment of length 6 units using ruler and mark two points on the drawn line segment by taking 2 units distance apart from both the end points. Then we can conclude that

(A) Line segment is divided into 3 equal parts
(B) Line segment is divided into 4 equal parts
(C) Line segment is divided into 5 equal parts
(D) None of these

19. Which two triangles have ∠B as common?

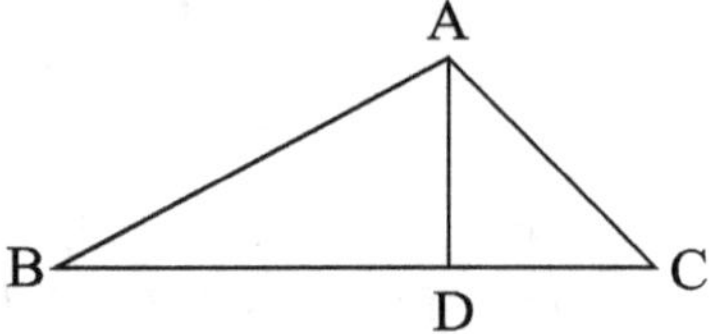

(A) Δ ABD and Δ ADC
(B) Δ ABD and Δ ABC
(C) Δ ABC and Δ ADC
(D) None of these

20. After observing the given figure, can you say B is equidistant from A and C?

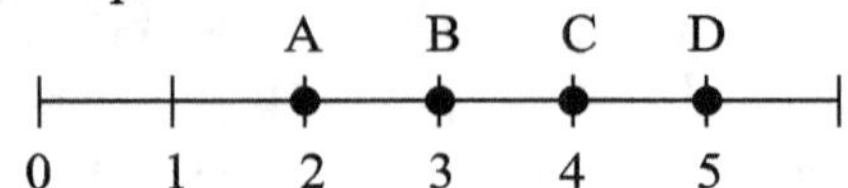

(A) Yes
(B) No
(C) Can't say anything
(D) None of these

HOTS (ACHIEVERS SECTION)

21. In Fig. which of the following is a regular polygon?

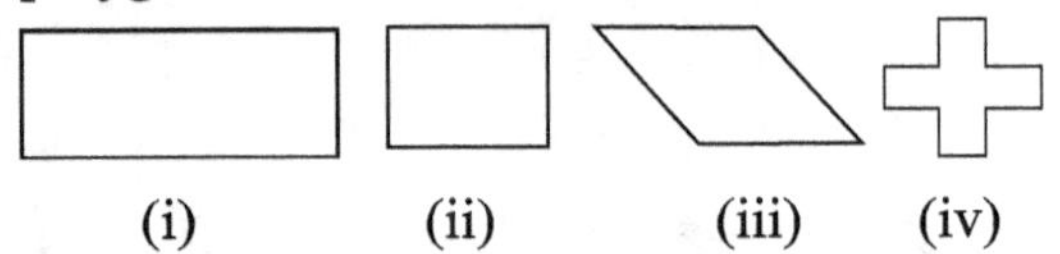

  (i)   (ii)   (iii)   (iv)

(A) (i)
(B) (ii)
(C) (iii)
(D) (iv)

22. In a triangle, one angle is of 90°. Then

(i) The other two angles are of 45° each
(ii) In remaining two angles, one angle is 90° and other is 45°
(iii) Remaining two angles are complementary

In the given option(s) which is always true?

(A) (i) only
(B) (ii) only
(C) (iii) only
(D) (i) and (ii)

23. The closed curve which is also a polygon is

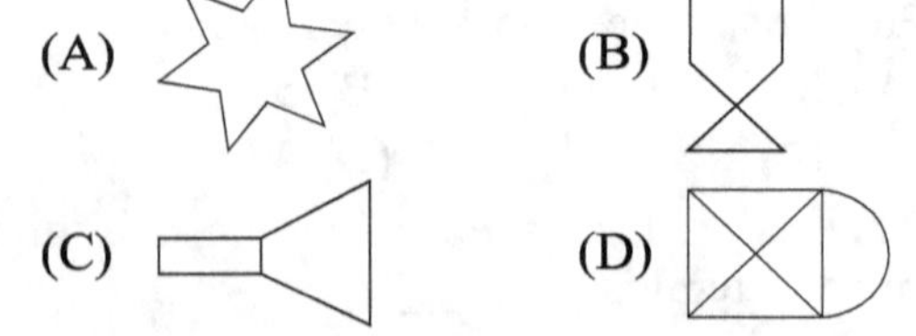

(A)   (B)

(C)   (D)

24. In a solid if $F = V = 5$, then the number of edges in this shape is
   (A) 6
   (B) 4
   (C) 8
   (D) 2

25. Which of the following cannot to be true for a polyhedron ?
   (A) $V = 4$, $F = 4$, $E = 6$
   (B) $V = 6$, $F = 8$, $E = 12$
   (C) $V = 10$, $F = 12$, $E = 20$
   (D) $V = 4$, $F = 6$, $E = 6$

1.	Ⓐ Ⓑ Ⓒ Ⓓ	6.	Ⓐ Ⓑ Ⓒ Ⓓ	11.	Ⓐ Ⓑ Ⓒ Ⓓ	16	Ⓐ Ⓑ Ⓒ Ⓓ	21.	Ⓐ Ⓑ Ⓒ Ⓓ
2.	Ⓐ Ⓑ Ⓒ Ⓓ	7.	Ⓐ Ⓑ Ⓒ Ⓓ	12.	Ⓐ Ⓑ Ⓒ Ⓓ	17.	Ⓐ Ⓑ Ⓒ Ⓓ	22.	Ⓐ Ⓑ Ⓒ Ⓓ
3.	Ⓐ Ⓑ Ⓒ Ⓓ	8.	Ⓐ Ⓑ Ⓒ Ⓓ	13.	Ⓐ Ⓑ Ⓒ Ⓓ	18.	Ⓐ Ⓑ Ⓒ Ⓓ	23.	Ⓐ Ⓑ Ⓒ Ⓓ
4.	Ⓐ Ⓑ Ⓒ Ⓓ	9.	Ⓐ Ⓑ Ⓒ Ⓓ	14.	Ⓐ Ⓑ Ⓒ Ⓓ	19.	Ⓐ Ⓑ Ⓒ Ⓓ	24.	Ⓐ Ⓑ Ⓒ Ⓓ
5.	Ⓐ Ⓑ Ⓒ Ⓓ	10.	Ⓐ Ⓑ Ⓒ Ⓓ	15.	Ⓐ Ⓑ Ⓒ Ⓓ	20.	Ⓐ Ⓑ Ⓒ Ⓓ	25.	Ⓐ Ⓑ Ⓒ Ⓓ

INTEGERS

LEARNING OBJECTIVES

➤ Basics of Integers

➤ Operations on Integers

MULTIPLE CHOICE QUESTIONS

1. $9 \times (-16) + (-12) \times (-16) = ?$
   (A) 48   (B) −48
   (C) 54   (D) −54

2. $(-12) \times 7 + (-12) \times (-4) = ?$
   (A) 32   (B) −32
   (C) −36   (D) 36

3. The sum of two integers is 65. If one of them is −47 what is the other number?
   (A) 112   (B) −112
   (C) 18   (D) −18

4. The difference of two integers is −27. If one of them is 32 then what is the other?
   (A) −59   (B) 59
   (C) 55   (D) −55

5. From the sum of 33 and −47, −84 is subtracted. What is the result?
   (A) 70   (B) −70
   (C) 94   (D) −94

6. $[37–(–6)] + [11–(–32)] = ?$
   (A) 86   (B) 74
   (C) −86   (D) −74

7. The sum of two integers is −27. If one of them is 265 then what is the other?
   (A) 292   (B) −292
   (C) 238   (D) −238

8. Subtract the sum of −1070 and 813 from 37.
   (A) 294   (B) −294
   (C) 272   (D) −274

9. What is the successor of −99?
   (A) −100   (B) −98
   (C) 100   (D) 98

10. What is the predecessor of −79?
    (A) −78   (B) −80
    (C) 78   (D) 80

11. What is the sum of −23, 62, −57 & 13?
    (A) −5   (B) 5
    (C) 15   (D) −15

12. What is additive inverse of −100?
    (A) 100   (B) 0
    (C) −1   (D) 1

13. $5 + (-2) + (-7) + 6 = ?$
    (A) 2   (B) −2
    (C) 3   (D) −3

14. $-2 + (-7) + 3 + (6) + (-9) + 11 = ?$
    (A) 4   (B) −2
    (C) 2   (D) −4

15. If −5 is added to 12 and result is subtracted from −7, which number is obtained?
    (A) −5   (B) 0
    (C) 14   (D) −14

16. Amir had ₹ 28760 in his bank account and his wife Laxmi had a debt of ₹ 12380. What was their combined net balance?

(A) ₹ 16380 (B) ₹ 14380
(C) ₹ 15380 (D) ₹ 17380

17. What is the value of $|-5 - 26 + 17|$?

(A) −14 (B) 14
(C) 48 (D) −48

18. What should be added to 57 to obtain −79?

(A) −136
(B) 136
(C) −22
(D) None of these

19. Subtract −2473 from the difference of 5396 and 7896.

(A) 27 (B) 4773
(C) 4973 (D) 4873

20. What will we get when −49 is added to the difference of 72 and −99?

(A) 76 (B) −76
(C) −21 (D) 122

21. What is the value of

$1 + (-473) + (-375) + (-383) + (-283) + 1700$

(A) 187 (B) 287
(C) 286 (D) 186

22. The sum of two integers is −307. If one of them is −173 what is the other ?

(A) 134 (B) −134
(C) 144 (D) −144

23. What is the value of $(-705) + 487 + (-317) + 265$?

(A) 270
(B) −270
(C) 370
(D) −370

24. Find the sum of predecessor of (−1709) and the successor of (−2305).

(A) 4014
(B) −4014
(C) 594
(D) None of these

25. Find the difference of negative of highest three digit number and smallest four digit number.

(A) 1
(B) −1999
(C) 1999
(D) None of these

26. Which one of the following is not correct?

(A) Successor of a number can be obtained by adding 1
(B) The difference between successor and predecessor of a number is smallest composite number
(C) Successor of greatest 5 digit number is smallest six digit number and predecessor of smallest 6 digit number is greatest 5 digit number
(D) The difference between lowest natural number and whole number is 1

27. $45 + 3 \times 2$ or $5 - (16 + 4) - 8 \div 4 = ?$

(A) 55
(B) 43
(C) 51
(D) Both (A) and (C)

28. Simplify the following

$6x^2 - 4x \div x$

(A) $6x - 4$
(B) $6x + 4$
(C) $4 + 6x$
(D) None of these

29. Find the product of the following fractions:

$$\frac{4}{3}, \frac{5}{7}, \frac{3}{2}$$

(A) $\dfrac{7}{3}$

(B) $\dfrac{10}{7}$

(C) $\dfrac{8}{3}$

(D) None of these

30. The product of the following fractions, 234.567 and 123.7 is?

(A) 29016.9372

(B) 29015.9373

(C) 29015.9379

(D) None of these

1.	Ⓐ Ⓑ Ⓒ Ⓓ	7.	Ⓐ Ⓑ Ⓒ Ⓓ	13.	Ⓐ Ⓑ Ⓒ Ⓓ	19	Ⓐ Ⓑ Ⓒ Ⓓ	25.	Ⓐ Ⓑ Ⓒ Ⓓ
2.	Ⓐ Ⓑ Ⓒ Ⓓ	8.	Ⓐ Ⓑ Ⓒ Ⓓ	14.	Ⓐ Ⓑ Ⓒ Ⓓ	20.	Ⓐ Ⓑ Ⓒ Ⓓ	26.	Ⓐ Ⓑ Ⓒ Ⓓ
3.	Ⓐ Ⓑ Ⓒ Ⓓ	9.	Ⓐ Ⓑ Ⓒ Ⓓ	15.	Ⓐ Ⓑ Ⓒ Ⓓ	21.	Ⓐ Ⓑ Ⓒ Ⓓ	27.	Ⓐ Ⓑ Ⓒ Ⓓ
4.	Ⓐ Ⓑ Ⓒ Ⓓ	10.	Ⓐ Ⓑ Ⓒ Ⓓ	16.	Ⓐ Ⓑ Ⓒ Ⓓ	22.	Ⓐ Ⓑ Ⓒ Ⓓ	28.	Ⓐ Ⓑ Ⓒ Ⓓ
5.	Ⓐ Ⓑ Ⓒ Ⓓ	11.	Ⓐ Ⓑ Ⓒ Ⓓ	17.	Ⓐ Ⓑ Ⓒ Ⓓ	23.	Ⓐ Ⓑ Ⓒ Ⓓ	29.	Ⓐ Ⓑ Ⓒ Ⓓ
6.	Ⓐ Ⓑ Ⓒ Ⓓ	12.	Ⓐ Ⓑ Ⓒ Ⓓ	18.	Ⓐ Ⓑ Ⓒ Ⓓ	24.	Ⓐ Ⓑ Ⓒ Ⓓ	30.	Ⓐ Ⓑ Ⓒ Ⓓ

OLYMPIAD WORKBOOK (IMO) CLASS— 6

FRACTIONS

6

➤ Types of Fractions

➤ Cross multiplication of fractions

MULTIPLE CHOICE QUESTIONS

1. A fraction equivalent to $\dfrac{2}{3}$ is

   (A) $\dfrac{2+3}{3+3}$

   (B) $\dfrac{2-1}{3-1}$

   (C) $\dfrac{2\times3}{3\times3}$

   (D) $\dfrac{2\div3}{3\div4}$

2. What should be added to $9\dfrac{2}{3}$ to get 19?

   (A) $9\dfrac{1}{3}$

   (B) $9\dfrac{2}{3}$

   (C) $8\dfrac{1}{3}$

   (D) $9\dfrac{1}{2}$

3. Which of the following is not a proper fraction?

   (A) $\dfrac{3}{4}$

   (B) $\dfrac{7}{8}$

   (C) $\dfrac{6}{11}$

   (D) $\dfrac{8}{5}$

4. Raju bought $7\dfrac{1}{2}$ litres of milk. Out of this milk $5\dfrac{3}{4}$ litres was consumed. How much milk is left with him?

   (A) $1\dfrac{3}{4}$ litre

   (B) $1\dfrac{1}{4}$ litre

   (C) $1\dfrac{1}{3}$ litre

   (D) None of these

5. What is the value of $6\dfrac{1}{2}-5\dfrac{2}{3}+3\dfrac{1}{4}$?

   (A) $1\dfrac{11}{12}$

   (B) $4\dfrac{1}{12}$

   (C) $3\dfrac{1}{12}$

   (D) $5\dfrac{1}{12}$

6. What is the value of $5-\dfrac{2}{3}-\dfrac{3}{4}$?

   (A) $4\dfrac{7}{12}$

   (B) $2\dfrac{7}{12}$

   (C) $3\dfrac{7}{12}$

   (D) None of these

7. What is the difference of $\dfrac{7}{8}$ and $\dfrac{5}{12}$?

   (A) $\dfrac{11}{12}$

   (B) $\dfrac{11}{16}$

   (C) $\dfrac{11}{24}$

   (D) None of these

8. What value is obtained when $1\dfrac{5}{6}$ is subtracted from 8?

(A) $5\dfrac{1}{6}$

(B) $6\dfrac{1}{6}$

(C) $3\dfrac{1}{6}$

(D) $7\dfrac{1}{6}$

9. What is the equivalent fraction of $\dfrac{3}{5}$ having numerator 21?

(A) $\dfrac{21}{34}$

(B) $\dfrac{21}{63}$

(C) $\dfrac{21}{49}$

(D) $\dfrac{21}{35}$

10. What is the equivalent fraction of $\dfrac{5}{12}$ having denominator 84?

(A) $\dfrac{25}{84}$

(B) $\dfrac{35}{84}$

(C) $\dfrac{30}{84}$

(D) $\dfrac{40}{84}$

11. What is the equivalent fraction of $\dfrac{56}{70}$ with numerator 4?

(A) $\dfrac{4}{15}$

(B) $\dfrac{4}{6}$

(C) $\dfrac{4}{5}$

(D) $\dfrac{4}{7}$

12. Which of the following is correct?

(A) $\dfrac{2}{3} > \dfrac{5}{6}$

(B) $\dfrac{4}{5} > \dfrac{2}{3}$

(C) $\dfrac{5}{7} < \dfrac{2}{3}$

(D) $\dfrac{6}{7} < \dfrac{4}{5}$

13. Which of the following is not correct?

(A) $\dfrac{2}{5} > \dfrac{1}{3}$

(B) $\dfrac{1}{4} > \dfrac{2}{3} < \dfrac{1}{4} > \dfrac{2}{3}$

(C) $\dfrac{4}{5} < \dfrac{6}{7}$

(D) $\dfrac{1}{7} > \dfrac{3}{5}$

14. A piece of wire is $3\dfrac{3}{4}$ m long broke into two pieces. One piece is $\dfrac{5}{8}$ m long, then what is the length of other piece?

(A) $2\dfrac{1}{8}$

(B) $3\dfrac{1}{8}$

(C) $4\dfrac{1}{8}$

(D) None of these

15. What should be added to $9\dfrac{2}{3}$ to get 40?

(A) $32\dfrac{1}{3}$

(B) $28\dfrac{1}{3}$

(C) $30\dfrac{1}{3}$

(D) $31\dfrac{1}{3}$

16. $3 + 1\dfrac{1}{5} - 2\dfrac{1}{3} + 2\dfrac{1}{5} = ?$

(A) $5\dfrac{1}{15}$

(B) $2\dfrac{1}{15}$

(C) $3\dfrac{1}{15}$

(D) $4\dfrac{1}{15}$

17. $5 - \dfrac{1}{2} + \dfrac{1}{3} - \dfrac{1}{4} = ?$

(A) $4\dfrac{7}{12}$

(B) $3\dfrac{7}{12}$

(C) $2\dfrac{7}{12}$

(D) $5\dfrac{7}{12}$

18. $7 + \dfrac{1}{5} - 2\dfrac{1}{3} + 4\dfrac{1}{2} = ?$

(A) $7\dfrac{11}{30}$

(B) $9\dfrac{11}{30}$

(C) $8\dfrac{11}{30}$

(D) $6\dfrac{11}{30}$

19. Which of the following is correct?

(A) $1\dfrac{1}{5} < 1\dfrac{1}{2} < 1\dfrac{3}{5} < 1\dfrac{3}{4}$

(B) $2\dfrac{1}{2} < 2\dfrac{1}{4} < 2\dfrac{1}{5} < 2\dfrac{1}{8}$

(C) $\dfrac{2}{3}<\dfrac{1}{2}<\dfrac{1}{4}<\dfrac{3}{4}$

(D) None of these

20. What should be added to $6\dfrac{2}{3}$ to get $8\dfrac{1}{2}$?

(A) $1\dfrac{5}{6}$

(B) $2\dfrac{5}{6}$

(C) $28\dfrac{1}{3}$

(D) $1\dfrac{1}{3}$

21. What should be subtracted from 5 to get $3\dfrac{2}{5}$?

(A) $1\dfrac{2}{5}$

(B) $1\dfrac{3}{5}$

(C) $2\dfrac{2}{5}$

(D) $2\dfrac{3}{5}$

22. $8\dfrac{1}{3}-7\dfrac{2}{5}+4\dfrac{2}{3}-6\dfrac{1}{5}=?$

(A) $\dfrac{3}{5}$

(B) $-\dfrac{3}{5}$

(C) $\dfrac{2}{5}$

(D) $-\dfrac{2}{5}$

23. $14-\left[12-\left\{9-\left(7-\overline{6-2}\right)\right\}\right]=?$

(A) 6

(B) 8

(C) 7

(D) 10

24. $\left[5\dfrac{1}{7}-\left\{3\dfrac{3}{10}+\left(2\dfrac{4}{5}-\dfrac{7}{10}\right)\right\}\right]$

(A) $\dfrac{9}{35}$

(B) $-\dfrac{9}{35}$

(C) $\dfrac{3}{35}$

(D) $-\dfrac{3}{35}$

25. $\dfrac{3}{4}$ of $\left(\dfrac{2}{3}-\dfrac{2}{5}\right)+\dfrac{1}{2}\div\dfrac{5}{2}=?$

(A) $\dfrac{1}{5}$

(B) $1\dfrac{1}{5}$

(C) $\dfrac{2}{5}$

(D) $2\dfrac{1}{5}$

26. What fraction of an hour is 12 minutes?

(A) $\dfrac{1}{5}$

(B) $\dfrac{1}{3}$

(C) $\dfrac{1}{6}$

(D) $\dfrac{2}{5}$

27. What is the value of P if
$$\dfrac{P-3}{2}-5=\dfrac{P-1}{3}+7$$

(A) 59

(B) 69

(C) 79

(D) 89

28. $5\dfrac{1}{2}-3\dfrac{2}{3}+7\dfrac{1}{5}-6\dfrac{1}{4}=?$

(A) $3\dfrac{17}{60}$

(B) $2\dfrac{47}{60}$

(C) $2\dfrac{57}{60}$

(D) $2\dfrac{41}{60}$

29. Which is the largest fraction among
$$\dfrac{4}{7},\dfrac{2}{3},\dfrac{1}{8},\dfrac{5}{6},\dfrac{7}{9}?$$

(A) $\dfrac{7}{9}$ (B) $\dfrac{5}{6}$

(C) $\dfrac{4}{7}$ (D) $\dfrac{2}{3}$

30. Which of the following fractions is the greatest $\dfrac{4}{7}, \dfrac{4}{9}, \dfrac{7}{8}, \dfrac{1}{3}$

(A) $\dfrac{4}{7}$

(B) $\dfrac{7}{8}$

(C) $\dfrac{4}{9}$

(D) None of these

1.	Ⓐ Ⓑ Ⓒ Ⓓ	7.	Ⓐ Ⓑ Ⓒ Ⓓ	13.	Ⓐ Ⓑ Ⓒ Ⓓ	19	Ⓐ Ⓑ Ⓒ Ⓓ	25.	Ⓐ Ⓑ Ⓒ Ⓓ
2.	Ⓐ Ⓑ Ⓒ Ⓓ	8.	Ⓐ Ⓑ Ⓒ Ⓓ	14.	Ⓐ Ⓑ Ⓒ Ⓓ	20.	Ⓐ Ⓑ Ⓒ Ⓓ	26.	Ⓐ Ⓑ Ⓒ Ⓓ
3.	Ⓐ Ⓑ Ⓒ Ⓓ	9.	Ⓐ Ⓑ Ⓒ Ⓓ	15.	Ⓐ Ⓑ Ⓒ Ⓓ	21.	Ⓐ Ⓑ Ⓒ Ⓓ	27.	Ⓐ Ⓑ Ⓒ Ⓓ
4.	Ⓐ Ⓑ Ⓒ Ⓓ	10.	Ⓐ Ⓑ Ⓒ Ⓓ	16.	Ⓐ Ⓑ Ⓒ Ⓓ	22.	Ⓐ Ⓑ Ⓒ Ⓓ	28.	Ⓐ Ⓑ Ⓒ Ⓓ
5.	Ⓐ Ⓑ Ⓒ Ⓓ	11.	Ⓐ Ⓑ Ⓒ Ⓓ	17.	Ⓐ Ⓑ Ⓒ Ⓓ	23.	Ⓐ Ⓑ Ⓒ Ⓓ	29.	Ⓐ Ⓑ Ⓒ Ⓓ
6.	Ⓐ Ⓑ Ⓒ Ⓓ	12.	Ⓐ Ⓑ Ⓒ Ⓓ	18.	Ⓐ Ⓑ Ⓒ Ⓓ	24.	Ⓐ Ⓑ Ⓒ Ⓓ	30.	Ⓐ Ⓑ Ⓒ Ⓓ

DECIMALS

LEARNING OBJECTIVES

➤ Like and unlike decimals
➤ Conversion of Decimals
➤ Comparison of Decimals
➤ Operations on Decimals

MULTIPLE CHOICE QUESTIONS

1. $8 + \dfrac{3}{10} + \dfrac{4}{100} + \dfrac{7}{1000}$

   (A) 8.347   (B) 8.0347
   (C) 8.3047   (D) 8.30047

2. $7\dfrac{1}{25} = ?$

   (A) 7.4   (B) 7.04
   (C) 7.004   (D) None of these

3. $6 - 0.23 + 1.2 - 5.76 = ?$
   (A) 1.21   (B) −1.21
   (C) 0.73   (D) 0.21

4. $37 - 35.79 = ?$
   (A) 1.31   (B) 1.21
   (C) 2.21   (D) 2.31

5. What is to be added to 74.5 to get 81?
   (A) 5.5   (B) 7.5
   (C) 6.5   (D) 7.5

6. What is to be subtracted from 7.3 to get 0.867?
   (A) 5.433   (B) 6.433
   (C) 7.433   (D) 6.233

7. By how much should 79.5 be decreased to get 27.89 ?
   (A) 53.61   (B) 52.61
   (C) 51.61   (D) 51.81

8. By how much should 32.754 be increased to get 53?
   (A) 20.246   (B) 20.346
   (C) 21.246   (D) 21.746

9. $76.3 - 7.666 - 6.77 - 5.55 = ?$
   (A) 56.341   (B) 56.314
   (C) 54.641   (D) 54.341

10. 37 mm = ?
    (A) 0.37 cm   (B) 0.037 m
    (C) 0.0037 m   (D) 0.307 cm

11. 2 kg 57 g = ?
    (A) 2.57 kg
    (B) 2.570 kg
    (C) 2.057 kg
    (D) None of these

12. During three days of a week, an auto driver earns ₹ 302.80, ₹ 379.20 and ₹ 297.60 respectively. What is his total earning during these days?
    (A) ₹ 979.60   (B) ₹ 978.60
    (C) ₹ 969.60   (D) ₹ 997.60

13. What is the decimal equivalent of $15\dfrac{17}{40}$?

    (A) 15.325   (B) 15.425
    (C) 15.375   (D) 15.725

14. Mohan purchased 5 kg 75 g of fruits and 3kg 465g of vegetables and put them in a bag. If this bag with these contents weights 9 kg. What is the weight of empty bag?

(A) 465 g   (B) 480 g
(C) 470 g   (D) 460 g

15. What should be subtracted from the sum of 4.902 and 15.376 to get 16.307 ?

(A) 3.791   (B) 3.971
(C) 2.971   (D) 4.971

16. The school bag of Sanjay and Rajesh weigh 6kg 40g and 7kg 207g respectively. By how much is Rajesh's bag heavier than that of Sanjay?

(A) 1 kg 167 g   (B) 1 kg 187 g
(C) 2 kg 167 g   (D) 1 kg 197 g

17. Which of the following is not in correct order?

(A) $3.72 > 3.67 > 3.05 > 3.03$

(B) $1.08 < 1.18 < 1.184$

(C) $3.502 > 3.067 > 3.126$

(D) $5.40 > 5.37 > 5.306$

18. The correct expanded form of 3.07 is

(A) $(3 \times 10) + \left(7 \times \dfrac{1}{10}\right)$

(B) $(3 \times 1) + \left(7 \times \dfrac{1}{10}\right)$

(C) $(3 \times 1) + \left(7 \times \dfrac{1}{100}\right)$

(D) None of these

19. Rasmi bought 2m 5cm cloth for her salwar and 3m 35cm cloth for her shirt. What is the total length of cloth bought by her?

(A) 5m 40cm
(B) 5m 45cm
(C) 5m 35cm
(D) None of these

20. The distance between Suman's house and office is 17km. She covers 9km 65m by scooter, 4 km 75m by bus and rest on foot. How much distance did she cover on foot?

(A) 3 km 960 m
(B) 2km 860 m
(C) 4km 860 m
(D) 3km 860 m

21. What number is obtained when 29.13 is subtracted from 73?

(A) 42.87   (B) 43.87
(C) 43.97   (D) None of these

22. Ritesh purchased a book worth ₹ 447.85 from a book seller and gave him a 1000 rupee note. How much balance did he get back?

(A) ₹ 552.25   (B) ₹ 553.15
(C) ₹ 552.15   (D) ₹ 551.15

23. Raman has ₹ 2000. He spent ₹ 439.75 for school fees, ₹ 208.75 for auto fare, ₹ 524.25, for books and rest for fooding. What is the cost of fooding?

(A) ₹ 817.25   (B) ₹ 837.25
(C) ₹ 827.25   (D) None of these

24. What is the sum of 0.3, 0.03 and 0.003?

(A) 0.999   (B) 0.393
(C) 0.636   (D) 0.333

25. Which is the smallest possible decimal fraction up to three decimal places?

(A) 0.101   (B) 0.000
(C) 0.001   (D) 0.011

HOTS (ACHIEVERS SECTION)

26. In covering 111 km, a car consumes 6 L of petrol. How many kilometers will it go in 15 L of petrol?

(A) 257.5 km   (B) 265 km
(C) 271.5 km   (D) 277.5 km

27. What is the value of $1 + 0.1 + 0.01 + 0.001$?

(A) 1.010   (B) 1.111
(C) 1.011   (D) None of these

28. $0.213 \div 0.00213 = ?$

(A) 10   (B) 100
(C) 1000   (D) $\dfrac{1}{10}$

29. What is the value of x if
$$\dfrac{144}{0.144} = \dfrac{14.4}{x} \text{ ?}$$

(A) 0.144   (B) 1.44

(C) 0.0144   (D) None of these

30. Find the value of $7\dfrac{3}{5} + 2\dfrac{1}{7} - 8\dfrac{1}{2} + 1$.

(A) 2.7   (B) 2.24

(C) 1.38   (D) 3.55

1.	Ⓐ Ⓑ Ⓒ Ⓓ	7.	Ⓐ Ⓑ Ⓒ Ⓓ	13.	Ⓐ Ⓑ Ⓒ Ⓓ	19	Ⓐ Ⓑ Ⓒ Ⓓ	25.	Ⓐ Ⓑ Ⓒ Ⓓ
2.	Ⓐ Ⓑ Ⓒ Ⓓ	8.	Ⓐ Ⓑ Ⓒ Ⓓ	14.	Ⓐ Ⓑ Ⓒ Ⓓ	20.	Ⓐ Ⓑ Ⓒ Ⓓ	26.	Ⓐ Ⓑ Ⓒ Ⓓ
3.	Ⓐ Ⓑ Ⓒ Ⓓ	9.	Ⓐ Ⓑ Ⓒ Ⓓ	15.	Ⓐ Ⓑ Ⓒ Ⓓ	21.	Ⓐ Ⓑ Ⓒ Ⓓ	27.	Ⓐ Ⓑ Ⓒ Ⓓ
4.	Ⓐ Ⓑ Ⓒ Ⓓ	10.	Ⓐ Ⓑ Ⓒ Ⓓ	16.	Ⓐ Ⓑ Ⓒ Ⓓ	22.	Ⓐ Ⓑ Ⓒ Ⓓ	28.	Ⓐ Ⓑ Ⓒ Ⓓ
5.	Ⓐ Ⓑ Ⓒ Ⓓ	11.	Ⓐ Ⓑ Ⓒ Ⓓ	17.	Ⓐ Ⓑ Ⓒ Ⓓ	23.	Ⓐ Ⓑ Ⓒ Ⓓ	29.	Ⓐ Ⓑ Ⓒ Ⓓ
6.	Ⓐ Ⓑ Ⓒ Ⓓ	12.	Ⓐ Ⓑ Ⓒ Ⓓ	18.	Ⓐ Ⓑ Ⓒ Ⓓ	24.	Ⓐ Ⓑ Ⓒ Ⓓ	30.	Ⓐ Ⓑ Ⓒ Ⓓ

DATA HANDLING

LEARNING OBJECTIVES

➤ Frequency
➤ Bar diagram
➤ Pictograph

MULTIPLE CHOICE QUESTIONS

Read the given bar graph and answer the questions given below

1. Which month maximum rainfall?

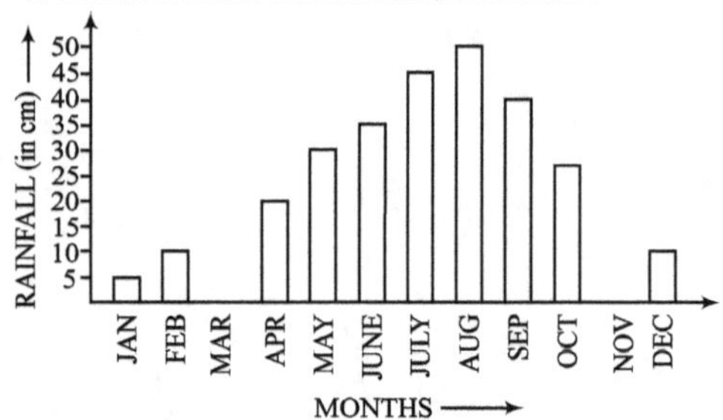

   (A) April   (B) July
   (C) August   (D) September

2. The given graph shows the marks scored by a student in his class test. Read the graph shown and answer the questions:

   Highest marks are scored in _______ .

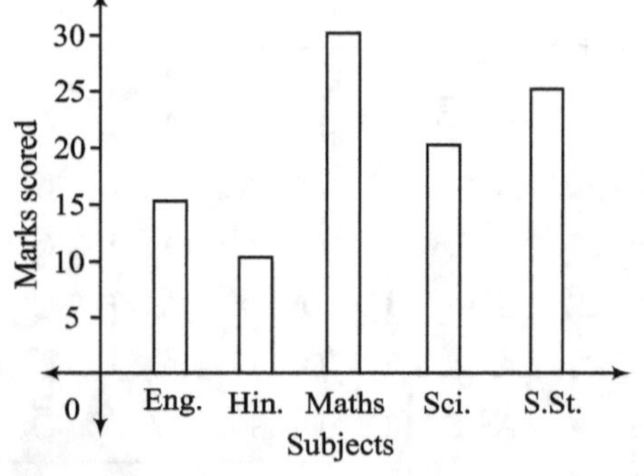

   (A) English
   (B) Hindi
   (C) Maths
   (D) None of these

3. The colours of refrigerators preferred by people living in a locality are shown in the following pictograph.

   Total number of people liked Blue and Green coloured refrigerators is _______ .

Colour of refrigerator	Number of People
Blue	👤 👤 👤 👤
Green	👤 👤 👤
Red	👤 👤 👤 👤 👤 👤
White	👤 👤

Key: 👤 = 10 People 👤 = 5 People

   (A) 70   (C) 60
   (C) 50   (D) 40

4. The colours of refrigerators preferred by people living in a locality are shown in the following pictograph.

   How many people liked Red coloured refrigerator?

Colour of refrigerator	Number of People
Blue	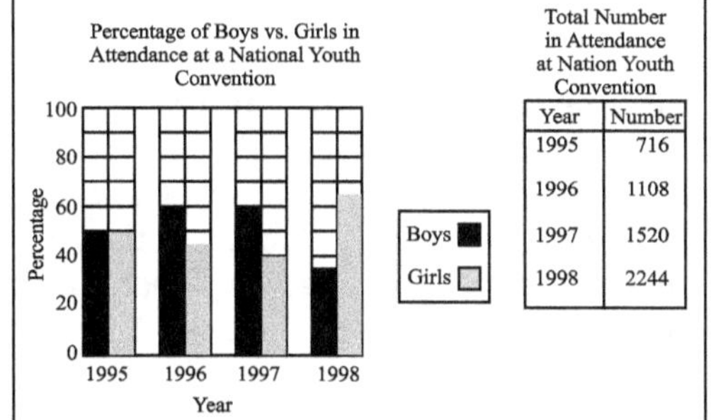
Green	
Red	
White	

Key: = 10 People, = 5 People

Total number of people liked Blue and Green coloured refrigerators is ______ .

(A) 40   (B) 30

(C) 20   (D) 55

5. How many boys attended the 1995 convention?

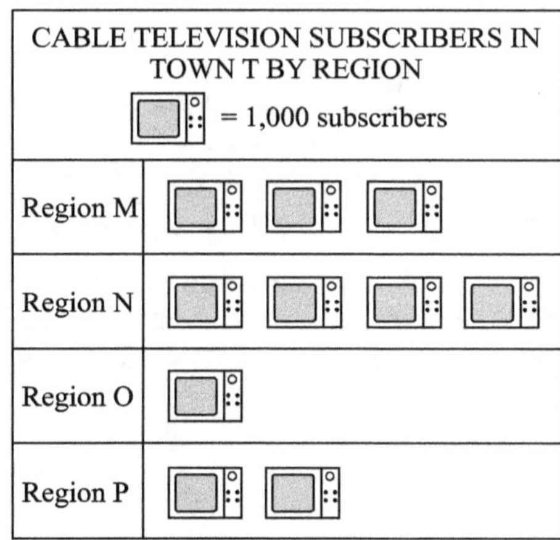

(A) 358   (B) 390

(C) 407   (D) 540

(E) 716

6. If the four regions shown in the graph above are the only regions in Town T, the total of which two regions accounts for exactly 70 percent of all cable television subscribers in Town T?

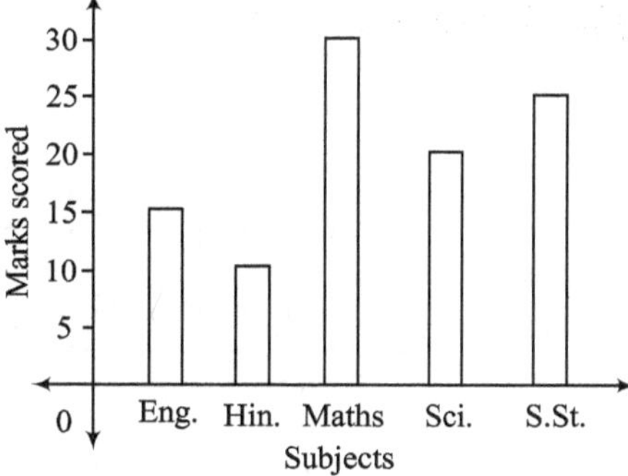

(A) Regions M and N

(B) Regions M and O

(C) Regions N and O

(D) Regions N and P

7. If in a pictograph, each diagram represents 18 students, then the number of students represented by 9 diagrams is

(A) 18/9   (B) 9/18

(C) 18×9   (D) 9/18

8. The following pictograph shows the number of scooters sold by a company during a week. Study the pictograph carefully and answer the questions given below.

Day	Number of scooters sold
Monday	
Tuesday	
Wednesday	
Thursday	
Friday	
Saturday	

Key: = 6 scooters

On which day of the week was the sale of the scooters was maximum?

(A) Monday   (B) Friday

(C) Tuesday   (D) Saturday

9. The given graph shows the marks scored by a student in his class test. Read the graph shown and answer the questions:

If the student wants to raise his total score upto 225, then how many more marks should he score?

(A) 125   (B) 100

(C) 200   (D) 25

10. **Directions For Questions**

The given graph shows the marks scored by a student in his class test. Read the graph shown and answer the questions:

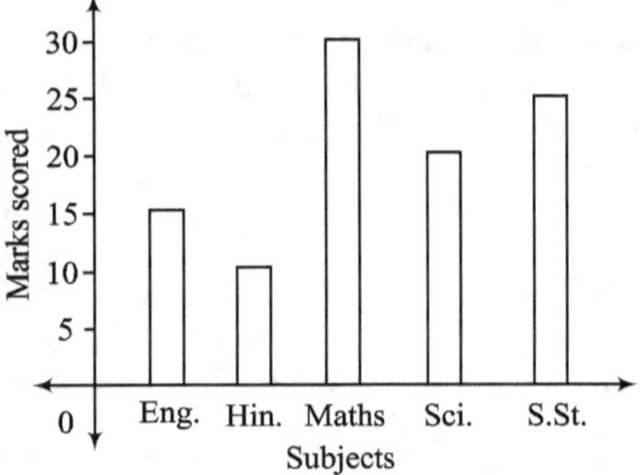

If the maximum number of marks is 50 in each subject, then in how many subjects student scored more than half of maximum marks?

(A) 1   (B) 2

(C) 3   (D) 4

11. Observe the adjoining bar graph, showing the number of one-day international matches played by cricket teams of different countries. Choose the correct answer from the given four options: How many more matches were played by India than Pakistan?

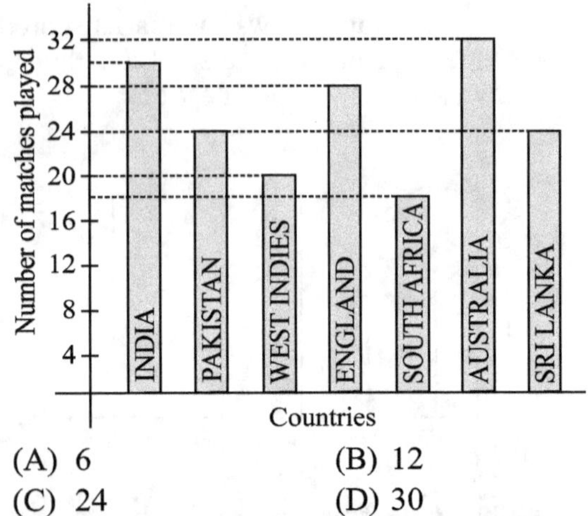

(A) 6   (B) 12

(C) 24   (D) 30

12. Observe the following pictograph which shows the number of ice cream cones sold by school canteen during a week. Chose the correct answer from the given options:

Day	Number of ice cream cones sold	= 2 cones
Monday	🍦🍦🍦🍦	
Tuesday	🍦🍦🍦🍦🍦🍦🍦	
Wednesday	🍦🍦🍦🍦🍦	
Thursday	🍦🍦🍦🍦	
Friday	🍦🍦🍦🍦🍦🍦	
Saturday	🍦🍦🍦🍦	

Ratio of the number of ice cream cones sold on Saturday to the number of ice cream cones sold on Wednesday is.

(A) 3 : 2   (B) 2 : 3

(C) 4 : 5   (D) 4 : 7

13. Observe the adjoining bar graph, showing the number of one-day international matches played by cricket teams of different countries. Choose the correct answer from the given four options: Which country played maximum number of matches?

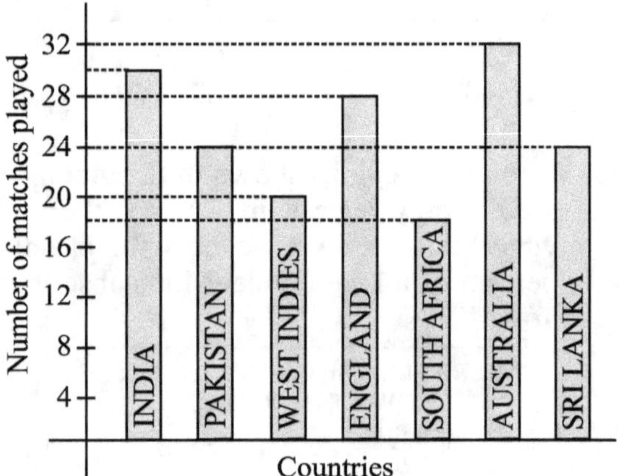

(A) India   (B) England

(C) Pakistan   (D) Australia

14. Observe the following pictograph which shows the number of ice cream cones sold by school canteen during a week. Chose the correct answer from the given options:

Day	Number of ice cream cones sold	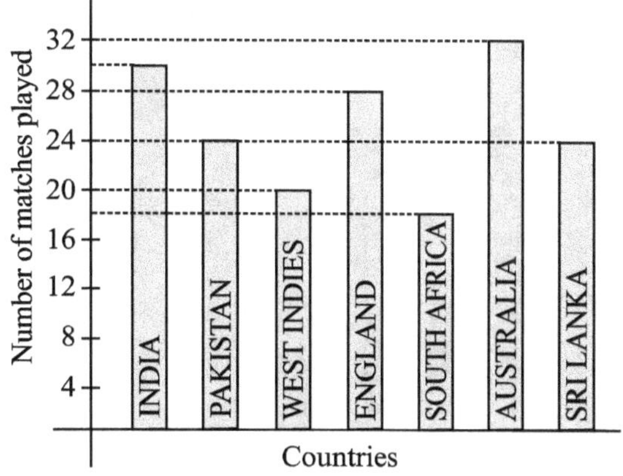 = 2 cones
Monday	🍦🍦🍦🍦🍦	
Tuesday	🍦🍦🍦🍦🍦🍦🍦🍦	
Wednesday	🍦🍦🍦🍦🍦🍦	
Thursday	🍦🍦🍦	
Friday	🍦🍦🍦🍦🍦🍦	
Saturday	🍦🍦🍦🍦	

Total number of ice cream cones sold during the whole week was:

(A) 33

(B) 67

(C) 65

(D) 57

15. Observe the following pictograph which shows the number of ice cream cones sold by school canteen during a week. Chose the correct answer from the given options:

Day	Number of ice cream cones sold	🍦 = 2 cones
Monday	🍦🍦🍦🍦🍦	
Tuesday	🍦🍦🍦🍦🍦🍦🍦🍦	
Wednesday	🍦🍦🍦🍦🍦🍦	
Thursday	🍦🍦🍦	
Friday	🍦🍦🍦🍦🍦🍦🍦	
Saturday	🍦🍦🍦🍦	

If the cost of one ice cream cone is Rs. 20, then the sale value on friday was:

(A) Rs.70

(B) Rs.140

(C) Rs.280

(D) Rs.1340

16. Observe the adjoining bar graph, showing the number of one-day international matches played by cricket teams of different countries. Choose the correct answer from the given four options.

Ratio of the number of matches played by India to the number of matches played by Sri Lanka is:

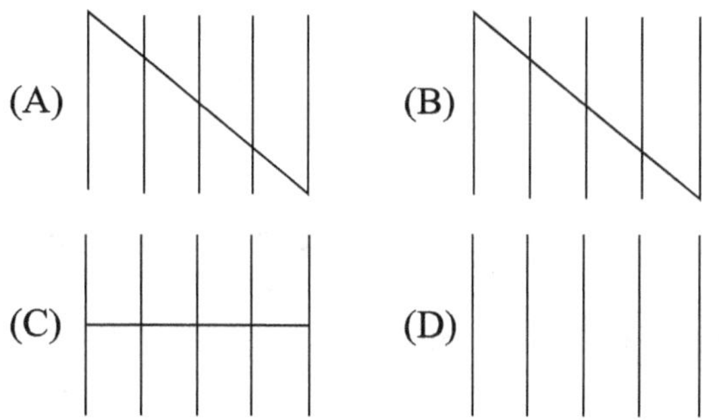

(A) 4 : 5   (B) 5 : 4

(C) 4 : 3   (D) 7 : 6

17. In tally mark, a group of five marks represented as ________ .

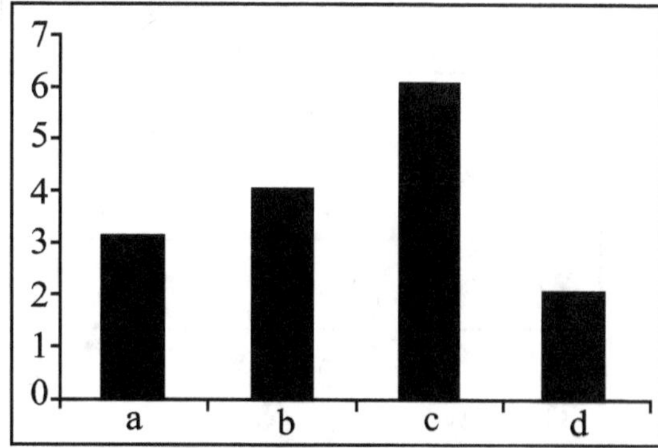

18. Examine the graph and determine which of the following is true.

(A) (c) minus (b) equals (b) minus (d)

(B) (a) plus (d) equals (c)

(C) (c) minus (d) equals (a)

(D) (a) plus (b) equals (c) plus (d)

19. Which two years did the least number of boys attend the convention?

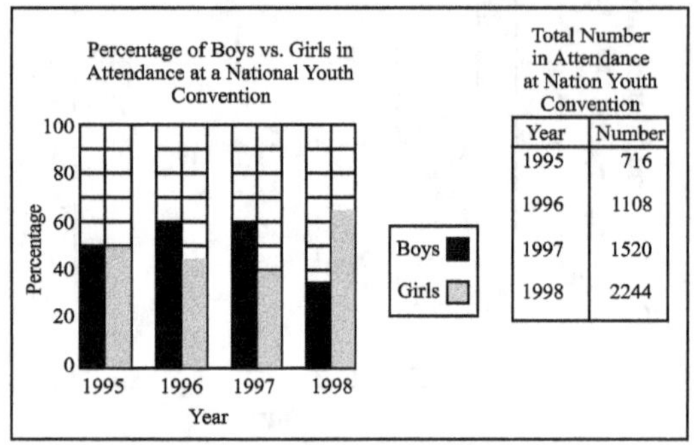

(A) 1995 and 1996
(B) 1995 and 1998
(C) 1996 and 1997
(D) 1996 and 1992

20. Jagadish surveyed the students of his school to determine their favourite sport. The results are shown in the graph.

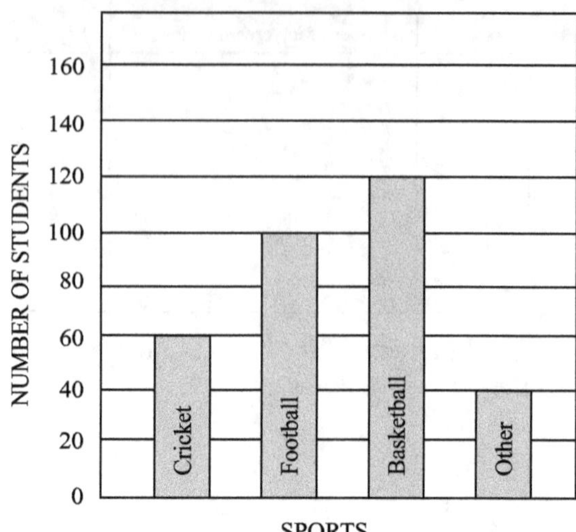

How many more students like Basketball than Cricket?

(A) 60   (B) 120
(C) 20   (D) 40

HOTS (ACHIEVERS SECTION)

21. The given pictograph shows the number of wall clocks sold by a company during a week. Each clock in the pictograph represents 5 wall clocks. How many more wall clocks were sold on Thursday than on Tuesday?

Day	
Monday	(4 clocks)
Tuesday	(5 clocks)
Wednesday	(3 clocks)
Thursday	(7 clocks)
Friday	(2 clocks)
Saturday	(1 clock)

(A) 9   (B) 8
(C) 5   (D) 10

22. Direction: The pictograph shows different subject books which are kept in a library. Observe the graph and answer the following questions.

Subject	Number of Books
Hindi	(6 books)
English	(8 books)
History	(2 books)
Science	(4 books)
Maths	(3 books)

1 (book) = 100 Books

How many English books are there in the library?

(A) 800   (B) 700
(C) 500   (D) 600

23. The bar graph shows the number of traffic accidents in a country from year 2000 to 2014. What is the difference between accidents in the year 2001 and 2004.

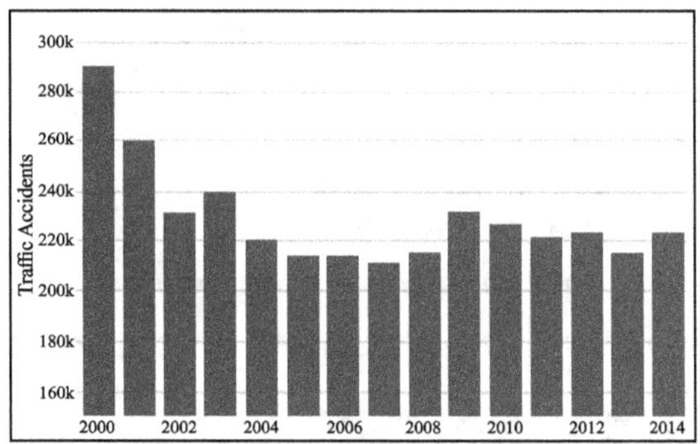

(A) 60,000   (B) 40,000

(C) 20,000   (D) 45,000

24. The given pictograph shows the number of wall clocks sold by a company during a week. Each clock in the pictograph represents 5 wall clocks. On what day was the sale maximum?

Monday	🕐🕐🕐🕐
Tuesday	🕐🕐🕐🕐🕐
Wednesday	🕐🕐🕐
Thursday	🕐🕐🕐🕐🕐🕐🕐
Friday	🕐🕐
Saturday	🕐

(A) Monday

(B) Tuesday

(C) Saturday

(D) Thursday

25. The given pictograph shows the number of students of class V participated in different games at Annual Diwali Mela. How many students tried the dart board?

Games	Number of students who participated
Ring the bottle	🏐🏐🏐🏐🏐
Dart board	🏐🏐🏐🏐🏐 🏐🏐🏐
Knock the stuff toy	🏐🏐🏐
Ring the prize	🏐🏐🏐🏐🏐 🏐🏐🏐🏐
Estimating weight	🏐🏐🏐
Each 🏐 stands for 17 students	

(A) 45

(B) 182

(C) 140

(D) 136

1.	Ⓐ Ⓑ Ⓒ Ⓓ	6.	Ⓐ Ⓑ Ⓒ Ⓓ	11.	Ⓐ Ⓑ Ⓒ Ⓓ	16	Ⓐ Ⓑ Ⓒ Ⓓ	21.	Ⓐ Ⓑ Ⓒ Ⓓ
2.	Ⓐ Ⓑ Ⓒ Ⓓ	7.	Ⓐ Ⓑ Ⓒ Ⓓ	12.	Ⓐ Ⓑ Ⓒ Ⓓ	17.	Ⓐ Ⓑ Ⓒ Ⓓ	22.	Ⓐ Ⓑ Ⓒ Ⓓ
3.	Ⓐ Ⓑ Ⓒ Ⓓ	8.	Ⓐ Ⓑ Ⓒ Ⓓ	13.	Ⓐ Ⓑ Ⓒ Ⓓ	18.	Ⓐ Ⓑ Ⓒ Ⓓ	23.	Ⓐ Ⓑ Ⓒ Ⓓ
4.	Ⓐ Ⓑ Ⓒ Ⓓ	9.	Ⓐ Ⓑ Ⓒ Ⓓ	14.	Ⓐ Ⓑ Ⓒ Ⓓ	19.	Ⓐ Ⓑ Ⓒ Ⓓ	24.	Ⓐ Ⓑ Ⓒ Ⓓ
5.	Ⓐ Ⓑ Ⓒ Ⓓ	10.	Ⓐ Ⓑ Ⓒ Ⓓ	15.	Ⓐ Ⓑ Ⓒ Ⓓ	20.	Ⓐ Ⓑ Ⓒ Ⓓ	25.	Ⓐ Ⓑ Ⓒ Ⓓ

MENSURATION

LEARNING OBJECTIVES

➤ Perimeter of Rectangle and Square ➤ Area of Rectangle and Square

MULTIPLE CHOICE QUESTIONS

1. If a wire of length 267 cm is bent to form an equilateral triangle, then what is the length of side of the equilateral triangle?
   (A) 69 cm   (B) 79 cm
   (C) 89 cm   (D) 99 cm

2. Mohit runs a distance of 7km 800m in going round a rectangular ground three times. What is the length of the ground if its width is 330m?
   (A) 670 m   (B) 770 m
   (C) 870 m   (D) 970 m

3. What is the perimeter of an isosceles triangle with equal sides 8.5cm each and third side 7cm?
   (A) 12 cm   (B) 24 cm
   (C) 13 cm   (D) 26 cm

4. What is the perimeter of regular hexagon having each side 6.5 cm ?
   (A) 39 cm   (B) 38 cm
   (C) 42 cm   (D) 46 cm

5. The cost of fencing a rectangular field at ₹ 18 per metre is ₹ 1980. If the width of the field is 23m, what is its length?
   (A) 36 m   (B) 24 m
   (C) 32 m   (D) 28 m

6. What is the diameter of the circle whose circumference is 66 cm?
   (A) 18 cm   (B) 21 cm
   (C) 23 cm   (D) 28 cm

7. What is the radius of the circle whose circumference is 264 cm?
   (A) 36 cm   (B) 42cm
   (C) 46 cm   (D) 48 cm

8. The diameter of the wheel of a car is 70 m. How many revolutions will it make to travel 1.65km?
   (A) $6\frac{1}{2}$ (B) $4\frac{1}{2}$
   (C) $7\frac{1}{2}$ (D) $5\frac{1}{2}$

9. What is the circumference of a circle whose diameter is 35cm?
   (A) 110 cm   (B) 120 cm
   (C) 105 cm   (D) 115 cm

10. The area of a rectangle is 630 cm² and its length is 35cm, what is its perimeter?
    (A) 102 cm   (B) 104 cm
    (C) 106 cm   (D) 108 cm

11. The total cost of flooring a room at ₹ 85/m² is ₹ 5100. If the length of the room is 8m, then what is its width?
    (A) 6.5 m   (B) 7.5 m
    (C) 8.5 m   (D) 8 m

12. The area of a rectangle is 540 cm². Its length is 36cm, what is its perimeter?
    (A) 92 cm   (B) 102 cm
    (C) 112 cm   (D) 118 cm

13. What is the area of square whose diagonal is $5\sqrt{2}$ cm?
    (A) 100 cm²　　　　　　(B) $25\sqrt{2}$ cm²
    (C) 25 cm²　　　　　　 (D) 50 cm²

14. The length and breadth of a rectangular park are in the ratio 5 : 3 and its perimeter is 128m. What is the area of the park?
    (A) 960 m²　　　　　　 (B) 1260 m²
    (C) 480 m²　　　　　　 (D) 680 m²

15. What is the number of square tiles of size 10cm required for decorating a wall of 12 m × 8 m?
    (A) 108000　　　　　　 (B) 9800
    (C) 9600　　　　　　　 (D) 9200

16. Five square flower beds each of side 3cm are dug on a piece of land 17cm long and 5cm wide. What is the area of remaining part of the land?
    (A) 35 cm²　　　　　　 (B) 40 cm²
    (C) 25 cm²　　　　　　 (D) 30 cm²

17. The perimeter of the given figure is 37 cm. find the missing value.

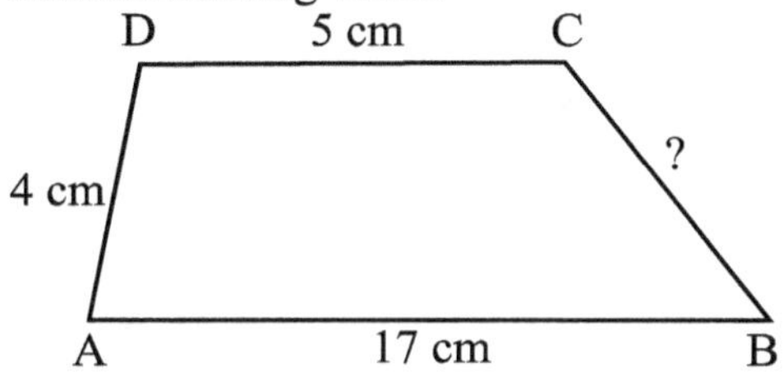

    (A) 10 cm　　　　　　　(B) 11 cm
    (C) 12 cm　　　　　　　(D) 13 cm

18. The area of a square is 2401 cm². What is its perimeter?
    (A) 184 cm　　　　　　 (B) 192 cm
    (C) 196 cm　　　　　　 (D) None of these

19. The diagonal of a square is $8\sqrt{2}$ cm what is its perimeter?
    (A) 32 cm　　　　　　　(B) 64 cm
    (C) 36 cm　　　　　　　(D) 42 cm

20. A floor is 7m long and 5m wide. A square carpet of sides 4m is laid on the floor. What is the area of floor that is not carpeted?
    (A) 15 m²　　　　　　　(B) 18 m²
    (C) 17 m²　　　　　　　(D) 19 m²

21. A room is 7m long and 4m 25cm wide. How many square metres of carpet is needed to cover the floor of the room?
    (A) 29.15 m²　　　　　 (B) 29.25 m²
    (C) 29.5 m²　　　　　　(D) 29.75 m²

22. Find the number of square tiles of size 15cm required for covering the floor of a room 9m long and 6m wide.
    (A) 1800　　　　　　　 (B) 2400
    (C) 1600　　　　　　　 (D) 2800

23. A rectangle and square are of equal area. The side of square is 18m. What is the length of rectangle if it is 12m wide?
    (A) 23 m　　　　　　　 (B) 27 m
    (C) 32 m　　　　　　　 (D) 22 m

24. What is the cost of tiling a rectangular plot of land 400m and 100m wide at the rate of ₹ 7 per sq. m?
    (A) ₹ 5614.285　　　　 (B) ₹ 5714.285
    (C) ₹ 5724.285　　　　 (D) ₹ 5734.285

25. If the length and breadth of a rectangle are doubled then its perimeter is
    (A) Halved　　　　　　 (B) Doubled
    (C) Tripled　　　　　　(D) None of these

26. The cost of fencing a square field at Rs. 35 per meter is Rs. 4480. What is area of the field?
    (A) 864 m^2
    (B) 964 m^2
    (C) 984 m^2
    (D) 1024 m^2

27. Length and breadth of a rectangle are 3.2 m and 150 cm. Then the area is
    (A) 48 sq cm
    (B) 4.8 cm^2
    (C) 4.8 sq m
    (D) 48 cm^2

28. A playground which is 250 m long and 20 m broad is to be fenced with wire. How much wire is needed?
    (A) 270 m
    (B) 230 m
    (C) 540 m
    (D) None of these

29. The length of a rectangle is 6/5th of its breadth. If its perimeter is 132 m, its area will be __________
    (A) 1,080 m^2
    (B) 640 m^2
    (C) 1,620 m^2
    (D) 2,160 m^2

30. The length of diagonal of a square whose area is 16900 m^2 is
    (A) 130 m
    (B) 130$\sqrt{2}$ m
    (C) 169 m
    (D) 144 m

Darken Your Choice with HB Pencil

1. Ⓐ Ⓑ Ⓒ Ⓓ	7. Ⓐ Ⓑ Ⓒ Ⓓ	13. Ⓐ Ⓑ Ⓒ Ⓓ	19. Ⓐ Ⓑ Ⓒ Ⓓ	25. Ⓐ Ⓑ Ⓒ Ⓓ
2. Ⓐ Ⓑ Ⓒ Ⓓ	8. Ⓐ Ⓑ Ⓒ Ⓓ	14. Ⓐ Ⓑ Ⓒ Ⓓ	20. Ⓐ Ⓑ Ⓒ Ⓓ	26. Ⓐ Ⓑ Ⓒ Ⓓ
3. Ⓐ Ⓑ Ⓒ Ⓓ	9. Ⓐ Ⓑ Ⓒ Ⓓ	15. Ⓐ Ⓑ Ⓒ Ⓓ	21. Ⓐ Ⓑ Ⓒ Ⓓ	27. Ⓐ Ⓑ Ⓒ Ⓓ
4. Ⓐ Ⓑ Ⓒ Ⓓ	10. Ⓐ Ⓑ Ⓒ Ⓓ	16. Ⓐ Ⓑ Ⓒ Ⓓ	22. Ⓐ Ⓑ Ⓒ Ⓓ	28. Ⓐ Ⓑ Ⓒ Ⓓ
5. Ⓐ Ⓑ Ⓒ Ⓓ	11. Ⓐ Ⓑ Ⓒ Ⓓ	17. Ⓐ Ⓑ Ⓒ Ⓓ	23. Ⓐ Ⓑ Ⓒ Ⓓ	29. Ⓐ Ⓑ Ⓒ Ⓓ
6. Ⓐ Ⓑ Ⓒ Ⓓ	12. Ⓐ Ⓑ Ⓒ Ⓓ	18. Ⓐ Ⓑ Ⓒ Ⓓ	24. Ⓐ Ⓑ Ⓒ Ⓓ	30. Ⓐ Ⓑ Ⓒ Ⓓ

ALGEBRA

LEARNING OBJECTIVES

➤ Basics of algebra
➤ Types of algebraic expression

➤ Polynomials

MULTIPLE CHOICE QUESTIONS

1. If $x = 4$, $y = -1$ and $z = -2$ then what is the value of $2x^2 - y^2 + 3z^2$?
   (A) 42
   (B) 43
   (C) 41
   (D) 45

2. What must be added to $5x^3 - 2x^2 + 6x + 7$ to make the sum $x^3 + 3x^2 - x + 1$?
   (A) $-4x^3 + 3x^2 - 6x - 7$
   (B) $-4x^3 + 5x^2 - 7x - 6$
   (C) $4x^3 + 3x^2 - 7x - 6$
   (D) None of these

3. By how much is $2x - 3y + 4z$ greater than $2x + 5y - 6z + 2$?
   (A) $8y - 10z + 2$
   (B) $-8y + 10z - 2$
   (C) $8y - 10z - 2$
   (D) $-8y + 10z + 2$

4. What is the simplified value of $2x - [3y - \{2x - (y - x)\}]$?
   (A) $4x - 5y$
   (B) $5x - 4y$
   (C) $5x - 6y$
   (D) $5x - 3y$

5. What is the value of m if
   $$\frac{2m}{3} + 8 = \frac{m}{2} - 1?$$
   (A) 54
   (B) -54
   (C) 52
   (D) -52

6. What is the value of x if
   $3(x + 6) + 2(x + 3) = 64$?
   (A) 8
   (B) 6
   (C) -8
   (D) 4

7. What is the value of p if
   $3(2 - 5p) - 2(1 - 6p) = 1$?
   (A) -2
   (B) -1
   (C) 2
   (D) 1

8. If 8 is subtracted from three times a number the result is 13. What is number?
   (A) 7
   (B) 5
   (C) 8
   (D) 9

9. The sum of three consecutive natural numbers is 114. Which is the greatest number?
   (A) 37
   (B) 38
   (C) 39
   (D) 41

10. The length of a rectangular field is 5m more than its breadth. If the perimeter of the field is 74 m, what is its length?
    (A) 16m
    (B) 17m
    (C) 21m
    (D) 23m

11. If 9 is added to twice a certain number, the result is 57, what is that number?
    (A) 38
    (B) 24
    (C) 46
    (D) 84

12. If 7 is subtracted from a number, we get 37, then, what is that number?
    (A) 42
    (B) 44
    (C) 46
    (D) 43

13. A man is thrice as old as his daughter. 5 years ago the man was four times as old as his daughter, what is the age of the daughter?
(A) 10 years
(B) 12 years
(C) 14 years
(D) 15 years

14. Karan's father is thrice as old as Karan. After 14 years his age will be twice that of his son. What is the age of Karan?
(A) 12 years
(B) 14 years
(C) 15 years
(D) 16 years

15. The sum of three consecutive even numbers is 78. Which number is smallest among them?
(A) 24
(B) 26
(C) 28
(D) None of these

16. Five times the price of a radio is ₹ 170 more than three times its price. What is the price of the radio?
(A) ₹ 85
(B) ₹ 95
(C) ₹ 105
(D) None of these

17. The length of a rectangular park is thrice its breadth. If the perimeter of the park is 168m, what is its breadth?
(A) 17m   (B) 21m
(C) 19m   (D) 23m

18. Kiran multiplies a certain number by 17 and adds 4 to the product, she gets 225. What is that number?
(A) 19   (B) 15
(C) 13   (D) 17

19. What is the sum of the expressions $3a - 2b + 5c$, $2a + 5b - 7c$ and $-a - b + c$?
(A) $4a - 2b + 2c$
(B) $4a + 2b - 2c$
(C) $4a - 2b - c$
(D) $4a + 2b - c$

20. What is the co-efficient of x^3 in $4y^2zx^3$?
(A) 4
(B) $4y^2$
(C) $4y^2z$
(D) None of these

21. What is the value of
$2a - [3b - \{a - (2c - 3b) + 4c - 3(a - b - 2c)\}]$
(A) $2b + 6c$
(B) $3b + 8c$
(C) $4b + 5c$
(D) $3b + 7c$

22. What is the value of
$xy - [yz - zx - \{yx - (3y - xz) - (xy - zy)\}]$?
(A) $xy - xz - 3y$
(B) $xy + 2xz - 3y$
(C) $xy - xz + 3y$
(D) None of these

23. What is the value of x if
$$\frac{x}{8} - \frac{1}{2} = \frac{x}{6} - 2 \text{ ?}$$
(A) 28   (B) 32
(C) 34   (D) 36

24. If a number is tripled and the result is increased by 7, we get 70 then what is the number?
(A) 21   (B) 23
(C) 24   (D) 27

25. A wire of length 86cm is bent in the form of a rectangle such that its length is 7 cm more than its breadth. What is its length ?
(A) 21 cm   (B) 23 cm
(C) 25 cm   (D) 27 cm

26. What must be subtracted from $a^3 - 4a^2 + 7a - 6$ to obtain $a^2 - 5a + 2$?

(A) $a^3 - 5a^2 + 12a - 8$

(B) $a^3 - 4a^2 + 2a + 8$

(C) $a^3 - 5a^2 - 12a + 8$

(D) None of these

37. What is the value of x if $16(3x - 5) - 10(4x - 8) = 40$

(A) 4   (B) 5

(C) 7   (D) 10

28. If $(a - b)$ is 6 more than $(c + d)$ and $(a + b)$ is less than $(c - d)$, then $(a - c)$ is

(A) 0.5   (B) 1.5

(C) 1   (D) −1

29. Which of the following equations has $x = 2$ as a solution?

(A) $x + 2 = 5$ (B) $x - 2 = 0$

(C) $2x + 1 = 0$ (D) $x + 3 = 6$

30. I think of a number and on adding 13 to it, I get 27. The equation for this is

(A) $x - 27 = 13$ (B) $x - 13 = 27$

(C) $x + 27 = 13$ (D) $x + 13 = 27$

—Darken Your Choice with HB Pencil—

1. Ⓐ Ⓑ Ⓒ Ⓓ	7. Ⓐ Ⓑ Ⓒ Ⓓ	13. Ⓐ Ⓑ Ⓒ Ⓓ	19 Ⓐ Ⓑ Ⓒ Ⓓ	25. Ⓐ Ⓑ Ⓒ Ⓓ
2. Ⓐ Ⓑ Ⓒ Ⓓ	8. Ⓐ Ⓑ Ⓒ Ⓓ	14. Ⓐ Ⓑ Ⓒ Ⓓ	20. Ⓐ Ⓑ Ⓒ Ⓓ	26. Ⓐ Ⓑ Ⓒ Ⓓ
3. Ⓐ Ⓑ Ⓒ Ⓓ	9. Ⓐ Ⓑ Ⓒ Ⓓ	15. Ⓐ Ⓑ Ⓒ Ⓓ	21. Ⓐ Ⓑ Ⓒ Ⓓ	27. Ⓐ Ⓑ Ⓒ Ⓓ
4. Ⓐ Ⓑ Ⓒ Ⓓ	10. Ⓐ Ⓑ Ⓒ Ⓓ	16. Ⓐ Ⓑ Ⓒ Ⓓ	22. Ⓐ Ⓑ Ⓒ Ⓓ	28. Ⓐ Ⓑ Ⓒ Ⓓ
5. Ⓐ Ⓑ Ⓒ Ⓓ	11. Ⓐ Ⓑ Ⓒ Ⓓ	17. Ⓐ Ⓑ Ⓒ Ⓓ	23. Ⓐ Ⓑ Ⓒ Ⓓ	29. Ⓐ Ⓑ Ⓒ Ⓓ
6. Ⓐ Ⓑ Ⓒ Ⓓ	12. Ⓐ Ⓑ Ⓒ Ⓓ	18. Ⓐ Ⓑ Ⓒ Ⓓ	24. Ⓐ Ⓑ Ⓒ Ⓓ	30. Ⓐ Ⓑ Ⓒ Ⓓ

RATIO AND PROPORTION

LEARNING OBJECTIVES

➤ Basics of ratio

➤ Unitary method

MULTIPLE CHOICE QUESTIONS

1. If 35 envelopes cost ₹ 87.50 how many such envelopes can we purchase for ₹ 315?
   - (A) 116
   - (B) 126
   - (C) 216
   - (D) 136

2. The weight of 65 magzines is 13 kg. What is the weight of 80 such magazines?
   - (A) 14kg
   - (B) 16kg
   - (C) 15kg
   - (D) 17kg

3. The boys and girls in a school are in the ratio 9 : 5. If the total strength of the school is 994, what is the number of girls?
   - (A) 355
   - (B) 365
   - (C) 375
   - (D) 385

4. The ratio of length of a field to its width is 5 : 3. What is the length if the width is 36 cm?
   - (A) 60cm
   - (B) 48cm
   - (C) 72cm
   - (D) 84cm

5. If ₹ 1020 is divided among A, B, C in the ratio 2 : 3 : 5, what is the share of C?
   - (A) ₹ 410
   - (B) ₹ 510
   - (C) ₹ 408
   - (D) ₹ 612

6. If ₹ 8100 is divided among L, M, N in the ratio 2 : 3 : 4, what amount does M receive?
   - (A) ₹ 4500
   - (B) ₹ 3600
   - (C) ₹ 1800
   - (D) ₹ 2700

7. A bus travels 183 km in 3 hours and a train travels 426 km in 6 hours. What is the ratio of their speeds?
   - (A) 51 : 71
   - (B) 61 : 71
   - (C) 61 : 73
   - (D) None of these

8. Raghav's salary of 7 months is ₹ 63000. What is his salary of 14 months?
   - (A) ₹ 12500
   - (B) ₹ 132000
   - (C) ₹ 12600
   - (D) None of these

9. If one dozen bananas cost ₹ 36, what is the cost of 26 bananas?
   - (A) ₹ 72
   - (B) ₹ 78
   - (C) ₹ 74
   - (D) ₹ 76

10. The cost of 2 kg of apples is ₹ 120. How many kilograms of apples can be purchased for Rs. 720 ?
    - (A) 8 kg
    - (B) 10 kg
    - (C) 12 kg
    - (D) 14 kg

11. Weight of 8 containers containing milk is 72 kg. What is the weight of 18 such containers?
    - (A) 152 kg
    - (B) 162 kg
    - (C) 142 kg
    - (D) 172 kg

12. The cost of two dozen oranges is ₹ 168. What will be the cost of 16 oranges?
    - (A) ₹ 96
    - (B) ₹ 124
    - (C) ₹ 102
    - (D) ₹ 112

13. Find the 1st term if 2nd, 3rd & 4th terms of a proportion are 12, 14 and 8 respectively.
   (A) 21
   (B) 24
   (C) 18
   (D) 28

14. What is the ratio of 40 cm to 1.5 m?
   (A) 4 : 15
   (B) 2 : 15
   (C) 3 : 5
   (D) 5 : 3

15. What is the value of x if
    $x : 92 :: 87 : 116$?
   (A) 76
   (B) 69
   (C) 96
   (D) 78

16. If 9, x, x, 49 are in proportion then what is the value of x?
   (A) 21
   (B) 23
   (C) 26
   (D) 31

17. If 25, 35, x are in proportion then the value of x is
   (A) 35
   (B) 49
   (C) 56
   (D) 63

18. In a proportion 1st, 2nd and 4th terms are 7, 42 and 72 respectively. What is the third term?
   (A) 8
   (B) 12
   (C) 14
   (D) 16

19. Ranjit earns ₹ 15300 and saves ₹ 1224 per month. What is the ratio of his income and expenditure?
   (A) 25 : 23
   (B) 27 : 25
   (C) 29 : 25
   (D) 31 : 29

20. Mahesh earns ₹ 16400 and his expenditure is ₹ 7400. What is the ratio of his saving and earning?
   (A) 41 : 83
   (B) 45 : 82
   (C) 47 : 81
   (D) 49 : 82

21. The ratio of income to expenditure of a man is 7 : 6. What is the saving if the income is ₹ 28000?
   (A) ₹ 9600
   (B) ₹ 8000
   (C) ₹ 6000
   (D) ₹ 4000

12. What is the ratio of 15 minutes to 2 hours?
   (A) 1 : 4
   (B) 1 : 6
   (C) 1 : 8
   (D) 1 : 10

23. What is the ratio of 210 grams to 7kg?
   (A) 3 : 10
   (B) 3 : 100
   (C) 3 : 1000
   (D) None of these

24. What is the ratio of 1.2km to 300m?
   (A) 8 : 1
   (B) 5 : 1
   (C) 4 : 1
   (D) 6 : 1

25. If $36 : x :: x : 16$, what is the value of x.
   (A) 18
   (B) 24
   (C) 16
   (D) 32

26. What is the share of B if Rs. 6900 is divided among A, B & C in the ratio 3 : 5 : 7?
    (A) 2100　　　　　(B) 2300
    (C) 2350　　　　　(D) 2400

27. The ratio of income to expenditure of Mohan is 7 : 5. What is the saving if the income is 14000?
    (A) Rs. 4000　　　(B) Rs. 4200
    (C) Rs. 4500　　　(D) 4600

28. The radius of a pencil is 6 mm and its length is 15 cm. What is the ratio of diameter of the pencil to the length of the pencil?
    (A) 2 : 25　　　　(B) 1 : 25
    (C) 3 : 25　　　　(D) 4 : 25

29. Express 568: 100 in its lowest term?
    (A) 142:25　　　　(B) 150:29
    (C) 234:19　　　　(D) 237:38

30. The sum of the digits of a three digit number is 19. If the digits of the numbers is in continued proportion and first two digits are 4 and 6 then find the third digit of the number.
    (A) 8　　　　　　(B) 7
    (C) 9　　　　　　(D) All of these

Darken Your Choice with HB Pencil

1.	Ⓐ Ⓑ Ⓒ Ⓓ	7.	Ⓐ Ⓑ Ⓒ Ⓓ	13.	Ⓐ Ⓑ Ⓒ Ⓓ	19	Ⓐ Ⓑ Ⓒ Ⓓ	25.	Ⓐ Ⓑ Ⓒ Ⓓ
2.	Ⓐ Ⓑ Ⓒ Ⓓ	8.	Ⓐ Ⓑ Ⓒ Ⓓ	14.	Ⓐ Ⓑ Ⓒ Ⓓ	20.	Ⓐ Ⓑ Ⓒ Ⓓ	26.	Ⓐ Ⓑ Ⓒ Ⓓ
3.	Ⓐ Ⓑ Ⓒ Ⓓ	9.	Ⓐ Ⓑ Ⓒ Ⓓ	15.	Ⓐ Ⓑ Ⓒ Ⓓ	21.	Ⓐ Ⓑ Ⓒ Ⓓ	27.	Ⓐ Ⓑ Ⓒ Ⓓ
4.	Ⓐ Ⓑ Ⓒ Ⓓ	10.	Ⓐ Ⓑ Ⓒ Ⓓ	16.	Ⓐ Ⓑ Ⓒ Ⓓ	22.	Ⓐ Ⓑ Ⓒ Ⓓ	28.	Ⓐ Ⓑ Ⓒ Ⓓ
5.	Ⓐ Ⓑ Ⓒ Ⓓ	11.	Ⓐ Ⓑ Ⓒ Ⓓ	17.	Ⓐ Ⓑ Ⓒ Ⓓ	23.	Ⓐ Ⓑ Ⓒ Ⓓ	29.	Ⓐ Ⓑ Ⓒ Ⓓ
6.	Ⓐ Ⓑ Ⓒ Ⓓ	12.	Ⓐ Ⓑ Ⓒ Ⓓ	18.	Ⓐ Ⓑ Ⓒ Ⓓ	24.	Ⓐ Ⓑ Ⓒ Ⓓ	30.	Ⓐ Ⓑ Ⓒ Ⓓ

SYMMETRY

LEARNING OBJECTIVES

➤ Bilateral symmetry
➤ Line of Symmetry
➤ Point Symmetry and Reflection Symmetry

MULTIPLE CHOICE QUESTIONS

1. How many lines of symmetries are there in rectangle?
   (A) 2 (B) 0
   (C) 1 (D) None of these

2. Find the number of lines of symmetry in regular hexagon.
   (A) 1 (B) 3
   (C) 6 (D) 2

3. How many lines of symmetries are there in regular pentagon?
   (A) 5 (B) 3
   (C) 4 (D) 2

4. How many lines of symmetries are there in a square?
   (A) 3 (B) 1
   (C) 2 (D) 4

5. How many lines of symmetries are there in a rhombus?
   (A) 4 (B) 2
   (C) 1 (D) 3

6. How many lines of symmetries are there in an isosceles triangle ?
   (A) 1 (B) 3
   (C) 2 (D) None of these

7. Which of the following letters have reflection line of symmetry about vertical mirror?
   (A) C (B) V
   (C) B (D) Q

8. How many lines of symmetries are there in an equilateral triangle?
   (A) 1 (B) 2
   (C) 0 (D) 3

9. Which of the following alphabets has line symmetry?
   (A) Z (B) A
   (C) Q (D) P

10. A parallelogram has ______ lines of symmetry:
    (A) 0 (B) 1
    (C) 3 (D) 2

11. Which of the following letters has both horizontal and vertical lines of symmetry?
    (A) A (B) W
    (C) O (D) D

12. Which of the following triangles is not possible?
    (A) Triangles with exactly one line of symmetry
    (B) Triangles with exactly two lines of symmetry
    (C) Triangles with exactly three lines of symmetry
    (D) Triangles with no line of symmetry

13. Which of the following letters of the English alphabet has no line of symmetry?
   (A) S   (B) A
   (C) H   (D) K

14. How many lines of symmetry are there in a regular hexagon?
   (A) 2   (B) 3
   (C) 4   (D) 6

15. What do you mean by symmetrical figures?
   (A) Figures with uneven balanced proportion
   (B) Figures with even unbalanced proportion
   (C) Figures without proportion
   (D) Figures with even balanced proportion

16. Which of the following statements is/are true?
   (I) The letter 'H' has both horizontal and vertical lines of symmetry.
   (II) The letter 'C' has no line of symmetry.
   (A) Both (I) and (II)
   (B) Neither (I) nor (II)
   (C) Only (I)
   (D) Only (II)

17. Which of the following shapes has infinite lines of symmetry?
   (A) Isosceles Triangle
   (B) Rectangle
   (C) Regular Pentagon
   (D) Circle

18. A rhombus has __________ line(s) of symmetry.
   (A) zero   (B) one
   (C) two   (D) four

19. Which of the following letters of the English alphabet has a horizontal line of symmetry?
   (A) F   (B) G
   (C) L   (D) X

20. Which of the following statements is/are true?
   (I) The letter 'x' looks the same as its mirror image.
   (II) The letter 's' looks the same as its mirror image.
   (A) Both (I) and (II)
   (B) Neither (I) nor (II)
   (C) Only (I)
   (D) Only (II)

HOTS (ACHIEVERS SECTION)

21. How many of the following letters have at least one line of symmetry?

OLYMPIAD

   (A) 3   (B) 4
   (C) 5   (D) 6

22. What is the smallest number of squares that must be added so that the line AB becomes the line of symmetry?

23. Which of the squares should be shaded to make the given figure symmetric?

   (A) 1   (B) 2
   (C) 3   (D) 4

(A) P and Q   (B) P and S
(C) Q and R   (D) R and S

24. Which of the following figures have at least two lines of symmetry?

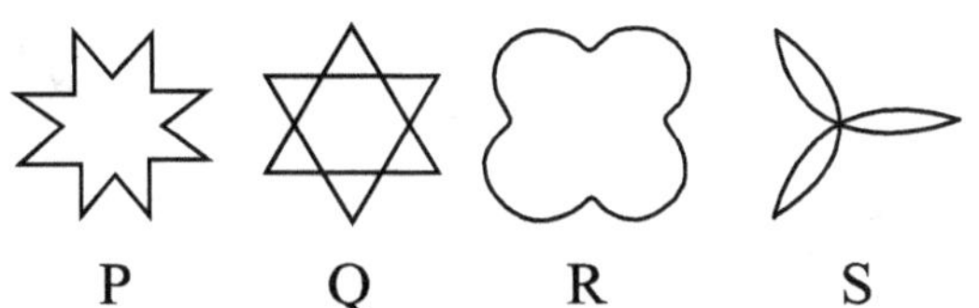

P   Q   R   S

(A) Only P
(B) Both P and Q
(C) Both Q and R
(D) P, Q, R and S

25. The minimum number of squares that must be shaded, so that the figure has a line of symmetry is __________.

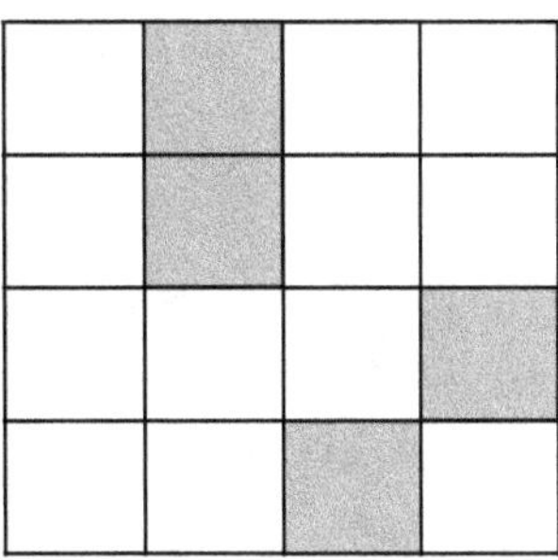

(A) 1   (B) 2
(C) 3   (D) 0

<hr>

1.	Ⓐ Ⓑ Ⓒ Ⓓ	6.	Ⓐ Ⓑ Ⓒ Ⓓ	11.	Ⓐ Ⓑ Ⓒ Ⓓ	16	Ⓐ Ⓑ Ⓒ Ⓓ	21.	Ⓐ Ⓑ Ⓒ Ⓓ
2.	Ⓐ Ⓑ Ⓒ Ⓓ	7.	Ⓐ Ⓑ Ⓒ Ⓓ	12.	Ⓐ Ⓑ Ⓒ Ⓓ	17.	Ⓐ Ⓑ Ⓒ Ⓓ	22.	Ⓐ Ⓑ Ⓒ Ⓓ
3.	Ⓐ Ⓑ Ⓒ Ⓓ	8.	Ⓐ Ⓑ Ⓒ Ⓓ	13.	Ⓐ Ⓑ Ⓒ Ⓓ	18.	Ⓐ Ⓑ Ⓒ Ⓓ	23.	Ⓐ Ⓑ Ⓒ Ⓓ
4.	Ⓐ Ⓑ Ⓒ Ⓓ	9.	Ⓐ Ⓑ Ⓒ Ⓓ	14.	Ⓐ Ⓑ Ⓒ Ⓓ	19.	Ⓐ Ⓑ Ⓒ Ⓓ	24.	Ⓐ Ⓑ Ⓒ Ⓓ
5.	Ⓐ Ⓑ Ⓒ Ⓓ	10.	Ⓐ Ⓑ Ⓒ Ⓓ	15.	Ⓐ Ⓑ Ⓒ Ⓓ	20.	Ⓐ Ⓑ Ⓒ Ⓓ	25.	Ⓐ Ⓑ Ⓒ Ⓓ

➤ Different Geometrical elements
➤ Angles and its types
➤ Types of triangles

MULTIPLE CHOICE QUESTIONS

1. How many lines can be drawn passing through two given points?
   (A) One
   (B) Two
   (C) Three
   (D) Unlimited number

2. A square has
   (A) One line of symmetry
   (B) Two lines of symmetry
   (C) Three lines of symmetry
   (D) Four lines of symmetry

3. A circle has
   (A) One line of symmetry
   (B) No lines of symmetry
   (C) An unlimited number of lines of symmetry
   (D) Two lines of symmetry

4. Which of the following statement is true?
   (A) A square has only two lines of symmetry
   (B) A parallelogram has no lines of symmetry
   (C) A rhombus has only four lines of symmetry
   (D) A rectangle has only four lines of symmetry.

5. A cuboid has
   (A) Length only
   (B) Thickness only
   (C) Length and breadth only
   (D) Length, breadth and height

6. The sum of all angles of a quadrilateral is
   (A) 180°　　　　(B) 270°
   (C) 360°　　　　(D) 540°

7. A quadrilateral having one and only one pair of parallel sides is
   (A) A kite
   (B) A rhombus
   (C) A trapezium
   (D) A parallelogram

8. How many sides does a triangle have?
   (A) 2　　　　(B) 3
   (C) 6　　　　(D) 9

9. The angles of a triangle are in the ratio 2 : 3 : 4. The smallest angle is
   (A) 40°　　　　(B) 60°
   (C) 80°　　　　(D) None of these

10. One of the base angle of an isosceles triangle is 65°. The vertical angle is
    (A) 40°　　　　(B) 50°
    (C) 65°　　　　(D) 35°

11. Each angle of an equilateral triangle is
    (A) 30°　　　　(B) 45°
    (C) 60°　　　　(D) 80°

12. An angle measuring 360° is
    (A) A straight angle
    (B) A complete angle
    (C) An obtuse angle
    (D) A reflex angle
13. The measure of a straight angle is
    (A) 60°   (B) 90°
    (C) 180°   (D) 360°
14. An angle measuring 205° is
    (A) An acute angle
    (B) An obtuse angle
    (C) A reflex angle
    (D) None of these
15. If there are 36 spokes in a bicycle wheel then the angle between a pair of adjacent spokes is
    (A) 10°   (B) 12°
    (C) 15°   (D) 18°
16. The maximum number of points of intersection of three lines in a plane is
    (A) 0   (B) 1
    (C) 2   (D) 3
17. Two planes intersect
    (A) In a plane
    (B) At a point
    (C) In a line
    (D) None of these
18. One of the acute angles of a right triangle is 55°. What is the other acute angle?
    (A) 45°   (B) 35°
    (C) 25°   (D) 55°
19. In a $\triangle ABC$, $3\angle A = 4\angle B = 6\angle C$. What is the measure of largest angle?
    (A) 80°
    (B) 60°
    (C) 40°
    (D) None of these
20. A triangle having sides of different length is called
    (A) A scalene triangle
    (B) A right triangle
    (C) An isosceles triangle
    (D) An equilateral triangle
21. The angles of a quadrilateral are in the ratio $3 : 4 : 5 : 6$. What is the largest angle
    (A) 80°   (B) 102°
    (C) 120°   (D) 150°
22. A quadrilateral having two pairs of equal adjacent sides but unequal opposite sides is
    (A) Square
    (B) Rectangle
    (C) Kite
    (D) Trapezium
23. A cone has how many vertex?
    (A) 1
    (B) 2
    (C) 3
    (D) None of these
24. A brick is an example of
    (A) Cube
    (B) Prism
    (C) Cylinder
    (D) Cuboid
25. How many vertex does a cylinder have?
    (A) 0   (B) 1
    (C) 2   (D) 3

HOTS (ACHIEVERS SECTION)

26. If there are 72 spokes in a bicycle wheel, then the angle between a pair of adjacent spokes is
    (A) 5°   (B) 10°
    (C) 12°   (D) 15°
27. The measure of two angles of a triangle are 67° and 43°. What is the measure of third angle?
    (A) 60°   (B) 65°
    (C) 70°   (D) 80°

28. In an isosceles $\triangle ABC$, the bisector of $\angle B$ and $\angle C$ meet at a point O. If $\angle A = 80°$ then what is the measure of $\angle BOC$?

   (A) 80°   (B) 130°

   (C) 100°   (D) 120°

29. If the diagonals of a quadrilateral bisect each other at right angle then the quadrilateral is a

   (A) Rhombus   (B) Rectangle

   (C) Kite   (D) None of these

30. What is the value of x in the given figure if $l \; // \; m$.

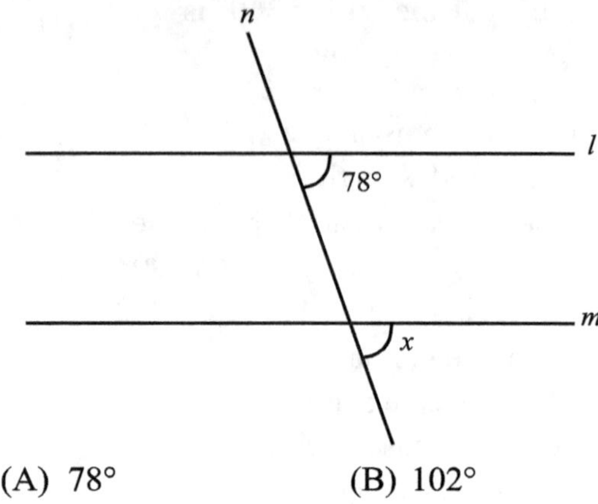

   (A) 78°   (B) 102°

   (C) 108°   (D) 94°

⏰ ⏰ ⏰

Darken Your Choice with HB Pencil

1.	Ⓐ Ⓑ Ⓒ Ⓓ	7.	Ⓐ Ⓑ Ⓒ Ⓓ	13.	Ⓐ Ⓑ Ⓒ Ⓓ	19	Ⓐ Ⓑ Ⓒ Ⓓ	25.	Ⓐ Ⓑ Ⓒ Ⓓ
2.	Ⓐ Ⓑ Ⓒ Ⓓ	8.	Ⓐ Ⓑ Ⓒ Ⓓ	14.	Ⓐ Ⓑ Ⓒ Ⓓ	20.	Ⓐ Ⓑ Ⓒ Ⓓ	26.	Ⓐ Ⓑ Ⓒ Ⓓ
3.	Ⓐ Ⓑ Ⓒ Ⓓ	9.	Ⓐ Ⓑ Ⓒ Ⓓ	15.	Ⓐ Ⓑ Ⓒ Ⓓ	21.	Ⓐ Ⓑ Ⓒ Ⓓ	27.	Ⓐ Ⓑ Ⓒ Ⓓ
4.	Ⓐ Ⓑ Ⓒ Ⓓ	10.	Ⓐ Ⓑ Ⓒ Ⓓ	16.	Ⓐ Ⓑ Ⓒ Ⓓ	22.	Ⓐ Ⓑ Ⓒ Ⓓ	28.	Ⓐ Ⓑ Ⓒ Ⓓ
5.	Ⓐ Ⓑ Ⓒ Ⓓ	11.	Ⓐ Ⓑ Ⓒ Ⓓ	17.	Ⓐ Ⓑ Ⓒ Ⓓ	23.	Ⓐ Ⓑ Ⓒ Ⓓ	29.	Ⓐ Ⓑ Ⓒ Ⓓ
6.	Ⓐ Ⓑ Ⓒ Ⓓ	12.	Ⓐ Ⓑ Ⓒ Ⓓ	18.	Ⓐ Ⓑ Ⓒ Ⓓ	24.	Ⓐ Ⓑ Ⓒ Ⓓ	30.	Ⓐ Ⓑ Ⓒ Ⓓ

LOGICAL REASONING

14

LEARNING OBJECTIVES

➤ Solving questions related to patterns

MULTIPLE CHOICE QUESTIONS

Study the pattern and find the missing number.

1.  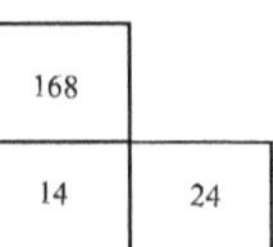 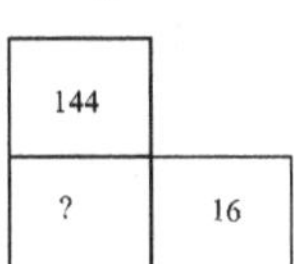

    (A) 14   (B) 16
    (C) 18   (D) 21

2. 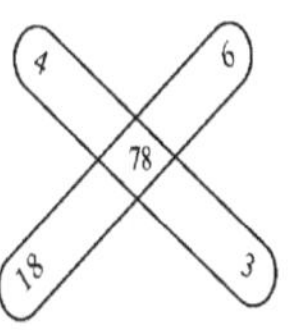 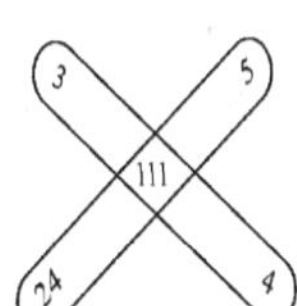 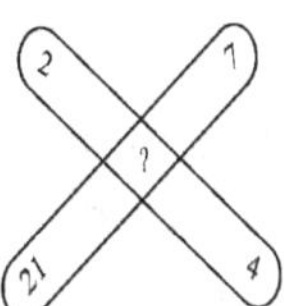

    (A) 98   (B) 96
    (C) 99   (D) 108

3. 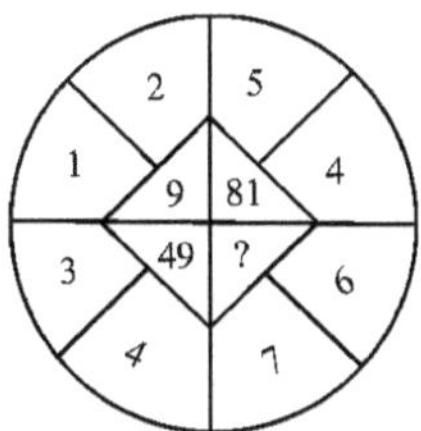

    (A) 121   (B) 149
    (C) 169   (D) 196

4. Physician : Treatment :: Judge : ?
    (A) Punishment   (B) Judgement
    (C) Lawyer   (D) Court

5. Ice : Coldness :: Earth : ?
    (A) Weight   (B) Jungle
    (C) Gravity   (D) Sea

6. Race : Fatigue :: Fast : ?
    (A) Food   (B) Laziness
    (C) Hunger   (D) Race

7. 67, 74, 81, 88, 95, ?
    (A) 101   (B) 102
    (C) 103   (D) 104

8. 109, 101, 94, 88, 83, ?
    (A) 78   (B) 79
    (C) 80   (D) 81

9. 9, 25, 49, 81, 121, ?
    (A) 141   (B) 144
    (C) 161   (D) 169

10.
    (A) History   (B) Physics
    (C) Civics   (D) Geography

11.
    (A) Mosque   (B) Temple
    (C) Mantery   (D) Church

12.
    (A) Operating system
    (B) Hard disk
    (C) Printer
    (D) Pendrive

13. If TRUTH is coded as SUQSTVSUGI, then the code for FALSE will be
(A) FGZBKNRTDF
(B) EGZBKMRDE
(C) EGZKMRTDF
(D) EGZBKMRTDF

14. In a certain code, INACTIVE is written as VITCANIE. How is COMPUTER written in the same code?
(A) UTEPMOCR
(B) MOCPETUR
(C) ETUPMOCR
(D) PMOCRETU

15. In a certain code, COVALENT, is written as BWPDUOFM and FORM is written as PGNS. How will SILVER be written in that code?
(A) MJTSFW
(B) MJTWFS
(C) KHRSFW
(D) None of these

16.
(A) Guarantee
(B) Group
(C) Groan
(D) Grotesque

17.
(A) Necessary
(B) Nature
(C) Naval
(D) Nautical

18.
(A) Foment
(B) Foetus
(C) Foliage
(D) Forceps

19. In the series given below, how many 8's are there each of which is exactly divisible by its immediate preceding as well as succeeding numbers?

2 8 4 3 8 5 4 8 2 6 7 8 4 6 2 8 4 1 7 ?
(A) 1
(B) 2
(C) 3
(D) 4

20. How many 5's are there in the following number sequence which are immediately preceded by 7 and immediately followed by 8?

7 5 5 8 4 5 7 8 4 5 9 8 7 5 8 7 8 4 3 2 5 8 7 6 ?

21. In the given series 7 4 5 7 6 8 4 2 1 3 5 1 7 6 8 9 2 how many pairs of alternate numbers have a difference of 2?
(A) 1
(B) 2
(C) 3
(D) 4

22. One morning after sunrise, Mohan was standing facing a pole. The shadow of the pole falls exactly to his right. Which direction was he facing?
(A) North
(B) South
(C) East
(D) West

23. If South – East is called East, North – West is called West, South – West is called South and so on what will North be called?
(A) South
(B) North East
(C) East
(D) North West

24. A, B, C and D are playing a game of carom. A & C and B & D are partners. D is to the right of C, who is facing West, then in which direction is B facing?
(A) East
(B) West
(C) North
(D) South

25. Knowledge
(A) School
(B) Teacher
(C) Textbook
(D) Learning

26. Culture
(A) Civility
(B) Education
(C) Agriculture
(D) Customs

27. Antique
(A) Rarity
(B) Artefact
(C) Aged
(D) Prehistoric

The options at top of second column belong to question 20:
(A) 1
(B) 2
(C) 3
(D) None of these

28. TERMINATE
   (A) TΣRMINATΣ
   (B) TERMINATE
   (C) TERMINATE
   (D) ETANIMRET

29. 1965INDOPAK
   (A) 1965INDOPAK
   (B) 1965INDOPAK

   (C) 1965INDOPAK
   (D) 1965INDOPAK

30. NATIONAL
   (A) NATIONAL
   (B) NATIONAL
   (C) NATIONAL
   (D) LANOITAN

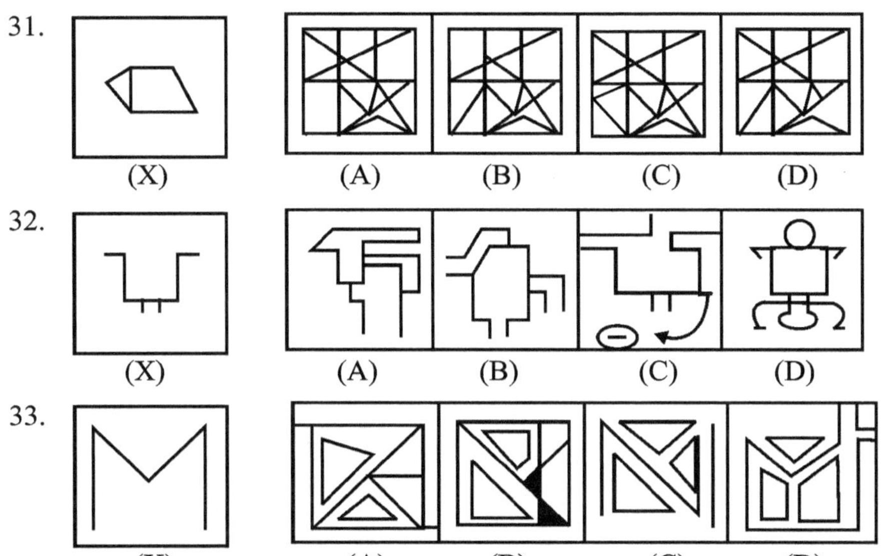

31. (X)   (A)   (B)   (C)   (D)

32. (X)   (A)   (B)   (C)   (D)

33. (X)   (A)   (B)   (C)   (D)

34. Which one will replace the question mark?

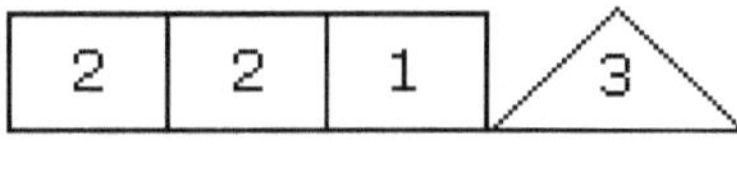

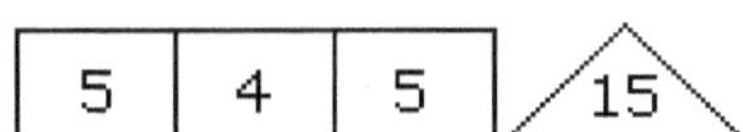

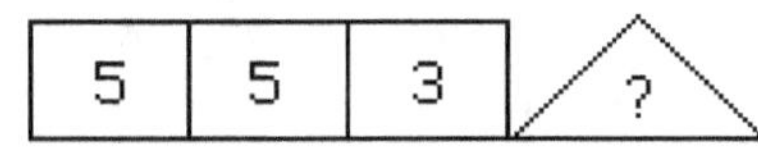

   (A) 11
   (B) 19
   (C) 15
   (D) 22

35. Which one will replace the question mark?

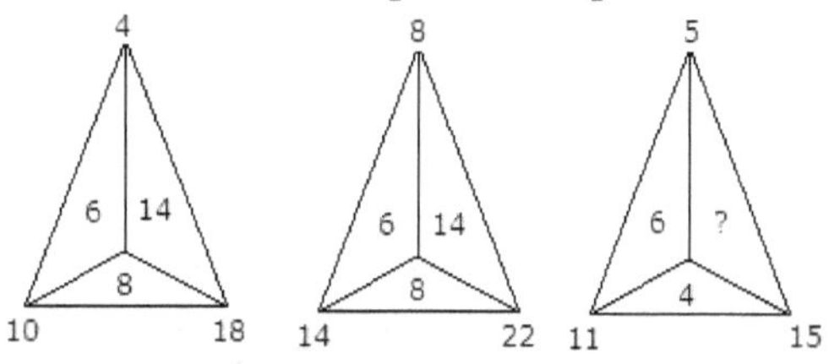

   (A) 8   (B) 14
   (C) 10   (D) 6

36. Which one will replace the question mark?

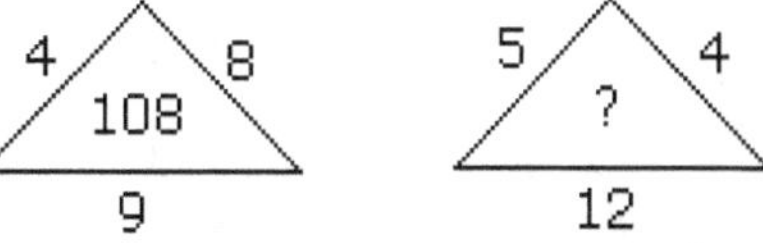

(A) 80

(B) 114

(C) 108

(D) None of these

37. Present ages of Sameer and Anand are in the ratio of 5 : 4 respectively. Three years hence, the ratio of their ages will become 11 : 9 respectively. What is Anand's present age in years?

(A) 24

(B) 27

(C) 40

(D) Can not be determined

38. A is two years older than B who is twice as old as C. If the total of the ages of A, B and C is 27, then how old is B?

(A) 7   (B) 8

(C) 9   (D) 10

39. A father said to his son, "I was as old as you are at present at the time of your birth". If the father's age is 38 years now, the son's age five years back was:

(A) 14 years

(B) 19 years

(C) 33 years

(D) 38 years

Darken Your Choice with HB Pencil

1.	A B C D	9.	A B C D	17.	A B C D	25.	A B C D	33.	A B C D
2.	A B C D	10.	A B C D	18.	A B C D	26.	A B C D	34.	A B C D
3.	A B C D	11.	A B C D	19.	A B C D	27.	A B C D	35.	A B C D
4.	A B C D	12.	A B C D	20.	A B C D	28.	A B C D	36.	A B C D
5.	A B C D	13.	A B C D	21.	A B C D	29.	A B C D	37.	A B C D
6.	A B C D	14.	A B C D	22.	A B C D	30.	A B C D	38.	A B C D
7.	A B C D	15.	A B C D	23.	A B C D	31.	A B C D	39.	A B C D
8.	A B C D	16.	A B C D	24.	A B C D	32.	A B C D		

MODEL TEST PAPER

1. If white is red, red is yellow, yellow is orange, orange is blue, blue is violet, violet is green, then what is the colour of brinjal?
   (A) Violet
   (B) Blue
   (C) Green
   (D) Yellow

2. If LAPTOP is written as NYRRQN then MOUSE is written as
   (A) OMVQG
   (B) OMWQG
   (C) OMWPG
   (D) ONWPG

3. If DELHI is coded as 451289 then what is the code for MUMBAI?
   (A) 132113219
   (B) 132113318
   (C) 122112219
   (D) 132013219

4. In the given sequence of numbers, how many times the number 7 is preceded by 3 and followed by 8?
   382372833782837873787382?
   (A) 1
   (B) 2
   (C) 3
   (D) 4

5. In a class of 35 students Kartik is placed 7th from the bottom whereas Mohit is placed 9th from the top. Sonal is placed exactly in between Kartik and Mohit. What is Kartik's position from Sonal?
   (A) 9th
   (B) 10th
   (C) 11th
   (D) 8th

6. Pointing to a photograph Arun said, "she is the mother of my brother's son's wife daughter." How is the lady related to Arun.
   (A) Cousin
   (B) Daughter in Law
   (C) Uncle
   (D) Brother in Law

7. Choose the odd one out from the following.
   (A) 29(96)17
   (B) 42(120)27
   (C) 77(76)68
   (D) 64(88)53

8. Choose the odd one from the given group.
   (A) Harbour
   (B) Coast
   (C) Oasis
   (D) Island

9. Choose the odd numeral group.
   (A) 1427
   (B) 3138
   (C) 5207
   (D) 3427

10. Manish walks 10m towards East and 20m towards South and 10m towards West. What distance and in which direction is he now from starting position?

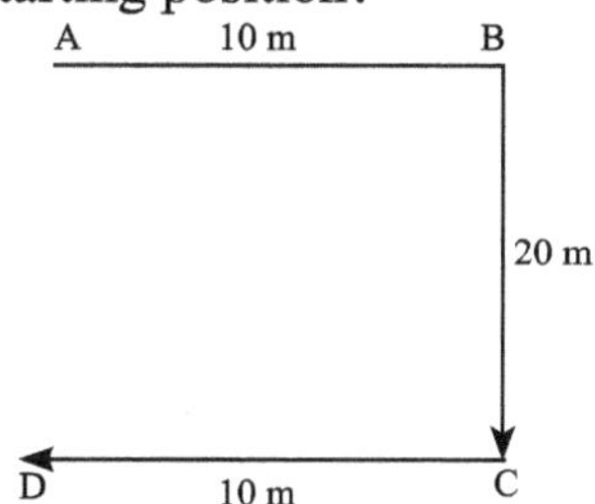

    (A) 20m North
    (B) 20m South
    (C) 20m West
    (D) 20m East

11. If X means +, Y means '—', Z means ÷ and P means '×' then what is the value of 10P2X5Y5?
    (A) 12
    (B) 20
    (C) 65
    (D) 30

12. How many 7's are there in the given sequence which are in between 2 and 5?
    82375642758275968257
    (A) 1
    (B) 2
    (C) 3
    (D) 4

13. If 5(16)3; 7(24)5 then 9(?)6
    (A) 43   (B) 44
    (C) 30   (D) 46

14. 17, 23, 29, 35 ?
    (A) 40   (B) 41
    (C) 42   (D) 43

15. If MAT = 34, DO = 19 then what is the value for MANGO?
    (A) 47   (B) 48
    (C) 49   (D) 50

16. X is the wife of 'Y' and "Y" is the brother of 'Z', 'Z' is the son of 'P'. How 'P' related to 'X'.
    (A) Sister   (B) Brother
    (C) Father-in-Law   (D) Aunt

17. If 213 = 419; 322 = 924; 415 = 16125 then 215 = ?
    (A) 4125   (B) 2541
    (C) 425   (D) 1625

18. If A is to the South of B and C is to the East of B, in what direction is A with respect to C?
    (A) North-East
    (B) North-West
    (C) South-West
    (D) South-East

19. If DRINK = 6, POLLUTION = 10, then GOVERNMENT is equal to?
    (A) 12   (B) 11
    (C) 10   (D) 8

20. Moon : Satellite : : Earth : ?
    (A) Planet   (B) Sun
    (C) Solar System   (D) Asteroid

21. Choose the word which is the least like the other words in the group
    (A) Copper   (B) Brass
    (C) Zinc   (D) Aluminium

22. Complete the series 13, 24, 46, 90, 178 __________.
    (A) 354   (B) 266
    (C) 364   (D) 344

23. Bihar is related to India in the same was as Florida is related to _________ ?
    (A) Canada   (B) North America
    (C) Mexico   (D) USA

24. If in a certain language, GRASP is coded as BMVNK, which word would be coded as CRANE
    (A) GVERI   (B) HWFSJ
    (C) EUDQH   (D) XMVIZ

25. Raman is 7 ranks ahead of Suman in a class of 39. If Suman's rank is seventeenth from the last, what is Raman's rank from the start?
    (A) 14th   (B) 15th
    (C) 16th   (D) 17th

26. Which is the largest of the fraction $\dfrac{2}{5}, \dfrac{4}{7}, \dfrac{3}{5}, \dfrac{6}{7}$?

    (A) $\dfrac{2}{5}$ (B) $\dfrac{3}{5}$

    (C) $\dfrac{4}{7}$ (D) $\dfrac{6}{7}$

27. What is the value of x if $\dfrac{1}{2} x + 7 = 19$
    (A) 5   (B) 12
    (C) 18   (D) 24

28. Two numbers are such that one of them exceeds the other by 9 and their sum is 81. Which is the larger number?
    (A) 36   (B) 45
    (C) 48   (D) 56

29. In an army camp there were provision for 423 men for 36 days. If 324 men attended the camp, how long did the provision last?
    (A) 42 days   (B) 43 days
    (C) 47 days   (D) 48 days

30. A bus covers 225 km in 3 hours and a train covers 600 km in 5 hours. What is the ratio of their speeds?
    (A) 3:5   (B) 5:7
    (C) 5:8   (D) 3:8

31. 20 boys can dig a pitch in 12 hours. How long will 16 boys take to do it?
    (A) 10 hours   (B) 15 hours
    (C) 18 hours   (D) 20 hours

32. How many lines can be drawn passing through two given points
(A) One
(B) Two
(C) Three
(D) Unlimited

33. What is the maximum number of points of intersection of three lines in a plane?
(A) 1
(B) 2
(C) 3
(D) 0

34. The cost of fencing a rectangular field at Rs 24 per meter is Rs 1920. If its length is 27 m then what is its breadth?
(A) 12 m
(B) 13 m
(C) 15 m
(D) 16 m

35. How many square tiles each of side 0.5 m will be required to pave the floor of a room which is 4 m long and 3 m broad?
(A) 48
(B) 44
(C) 56
(D) 60

36. A brick is an example of a
(A) Cube
(B) Cuboid
(C) Cylinder
(D) Prism

37. The angles of a quadrilateral are 3:4:5:6. What is the difference of largest and smallest angle of quadrilateral?
(A) 20°
(B) 30°
(C) 40°
(D) 60°

38. In an isosceles $\triangle$ ABC, the bisectors of $\angle$B & $\angle$C meet at a point O. If $\angle$A = 40° then $\angle$BOC = ?
(A) 80°
(B) 90°
(C) 100°
(D) 110°

39. In the adjoining figure if $\angle$D + $\angle$E = 105°. What is the value of $\angle$F.

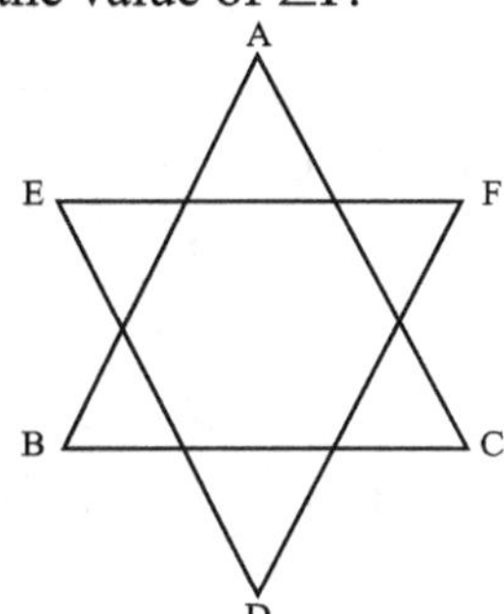

40. The ratio of length of a field to its width is 5:3. What is its length if the width is 42 m?
(A) 60 m
(B) 65 m
(C) 70 m
(D) 72 m

41. If $144 : x :: x : 121$ then what is the value of x ?
(A) 112
(B) 122
(C) 132
(D) 142

42. The cost of 5 bananas is Rs. 25. Then what is the cost of 5 dozen bananas?
(A) Rs. 200
(B) Rs. 240
(C) Rs. 280
(D) Rs. 300

43. What is the value of x if $\dfrac{x}{8} - \dfrac{1}{2} = \dfrac{x}{6} - 2$?
(A) 28
(B) 32
(C) 36
(D) 40

44. What is the value of P if $3(2 - 5P) - 2(1 - 6P) = 1$?
(A) 1
(B) $\dfrac{1}{2}$
(C) $\dfrac{1}{3}$
(D) 2

45. What must be subtracted from $a^2 - 3a + 5$ to obtain $5a^2 - 7a + 9$?
(A) $-3a^2 + 4a + 4$
(B) $-4a^2 + 4a - 4$
(C) $4a^2 - 4a + 4$
(D) None of these

46. By how much does 5 exceed $5x - 7y - 7$?
(A) $-5x + 7y + 12$
(B) $5x - 7y - 12$
(C) $5x - 7y$
(D) None of these

47. What is the co-efficient of a^2bc in $-6xba^2c$?
(A) –6
(B) $-6x$
(C) $-6bx$
(D) $-6abc$

48. Among 2.007, 2.067, 2.607 and 2.67 which is the largest?

    (A) 2.607   (B) 2.67

    (C) 2.007   (D) 2.067

49. $0.404 + 0.004 + 4.044 + 4.444 = ?$

    (A) 8.896   (B) 8.886

    (C) 8.096   (D) 8.806

50. The length of a rectangular hall is 5 m more than its breadth. If the perimeter is 74 m. What is the area of rectangle?

    (A) $332m^2$

    (B) $334m^2$

    (C) $336m^2$

    (D) $338m^2$

Darken Your Choice with HB Pencil

	A B C D		A B C D		A B C D		A B C D		A B C D
1.	Ⓐ Ⓑ Ⓒ Ⓓ	11.	Ⓐ Ⓑ Ⓒ Ⓓ	21.	Ⓐ Ⓑ Ⓒ Ⓓ	31.	Ⓐ Ⓑ Ⓒ Ⓓ	41.	Ⓐ Ⓑ Ⓒ Ⓓ
2.	Ⓐ Ⓑ Ⓒ Ⓓ	12.	Ⓐ Ⓑ Ⓒ Ⓓ	22.	Ⓐ Ⓑ Ⓒ Ⓓ	32.	Ⓐ Ⓑ Ⓒ Ⓓ	42.	Ⓐ Ⓑ Ⓒ Ⓓ
3.	Ⓐ Ⓑ Ⓒ Ⓓ	13.	Ⓐ Ⓑ Ⓒ Ⓓ	23.	Ⓐ Ⓑ Ⓒ Ⓓ	33.	Ⓐ Ⓑ Ⓒ Ⓓ	43.	Ⓐ Ⓑ Ⓒ Ⓓ
4.	Ⓐ Ⓑ Ⓒ Ⓓ	14.	Ⓐ Ⓑ Ⓒ Ⓓ	24.	Ⓐ Ⓑ Ⓒ Ⓓ	34.	Ⓐ Ⓑ Ⓒ Ⓓ	44.	Ⓐ Ⓑ Ⓒ Ⓓ
5.	Ⓐ Ⓑ Ⓒ Ⓓ	15.	Ⓐ Ⓑ Ⓒ Ⓓ	25.	Ⓐ Ⓑ Ⓒ Ⓓ	35.	Ⓐ Ⓑ Ⓒ Ⓓ	45.	Ⓐ Ⓑ Ⓒ Ⓓ
6.	Ⓐ Ⓑ Ⓒ Ⓓ	16.	Ⓐ Ⓑ Ⓒ Ⓓ	26.	Ⓐ Ⓑ Ⓒ Ⓓ	36.	Ⓐ Ⓑ Ⓒ Ⓓ	46.	Ⓐ Ⓑ Ⓒ Ⓓ
7.	Ⓐ Ⓑ Ⓒ Ⓓ	17.	Ⓐ Ⓑ Ⓒ Ⓓ	27.	Ⓐ Ⓑ Ⓒ Ⓓ	37.	Ⓐ Ⓑ Ⓒ Ⓓ	47.	Ⓐ Ⓑ Ⓒ Ⓓ
8.	Ⓐ Ⓑ Ⓒ Ⓓ	18.	Ⓐ Ⓑ Ⓒ Ⓓ	28.	Ⓐ Ⓑ Ⓒ Ⓓ	38.	Ⓐ Ⓑ Ⓒ Ⓓ	48.	Ⓐ Ⓑ Ⓒ Ⓓ
9.	Ⓐ Ⓑ Ⓒ Ⓓ	19.	Ⓐ Ⓑ Ⓒ Ⓓ	29.	Ⓐ Ⓑ Ⓒ Ⓓ	39.	Ⓐ Ⓑ Ⓒ Ⓓ	49.	Ⓐ Ⓑ Ⓒ Ⓓ
10.	Ⓐ Ⓑ Ⓒ Ⓓ	20.	Ⓐ Ⓑ Ⓒ Ⓓ	30.	Ⓐ Ⓑ Ⓒ Ⓓ	40.	Ⓐ Ⓑ Ⓒ Ⓓ	50.	Ⓐ Ⓑ Ⓒ Ⓓ

HINTS AND SOLUTIONS

Answer Key

1. (B)	2. (D)	3. (A)	4. (B)	5. (B)	6. (C)	7. (A)	8. (C)	9. (D)	10. (A)
11. (C)	12. (B)	13. (A)	14. (A)	15. (B)	16. (A)	17. (A)	18. (D)	19. (B)	20. (D)
21. (C)	22. (B)	23. (B)	24. (C)	25. (B)					

1. (B)

Round off of 43×78
$$= 40 \times 80 = 3200$$

2. (D)

$1101010 - 336414$
$$= 764596$$

3. (A)

Increase in population $= 18002403 - 14693675$
$$= 3308728$$

4. (B)

Numbers in ascending order are 3279, 3287, 3307, (3379), 3467, 3502, 3667.

5. (B)

Cloth required for 4 shirts $= \dfrac{44}{16} \times 4 = 11\text{m}$

6. (C)

Length of each piece $= \dfrac{20}{8} = 2.5\text{m}$

7. (A)

$10000000 - 5943679 = 4056321$

8. (C)

Required amount $= 8719 \times 12 \times 12$
$$= ₹\ 1255536$$

9. (D)

Required amount $= 49735 \times 487$
$$= ₹\ 24220945$$

10. (A)

Cost of each flat $= \dfrac{68251500}{18} = ₹\ 3791750$

11. (C)

Required difference $= 867 - 768 = 99$

12. (B)

Required value $= 387 + 783 = 1170$

13. (A)

$XCII = (100 - 10) + 1 + 1 = 92$

14. (A)

XXXX is meaningless.

15. (B)

$CDXLVI = (500 - 100) + (50 - 10) + 5 + 1$
$$= 400 + 40 + 6$$
$$= 446$$

16. (A)

Required difference $= 70 - 7 = 63$

17. (A)

Speed of the car $= \dfrac{\text{distance}}{\text{time}} = \dfrac{570}{16}$
$$= 35.625 \text{ km/hr.}$$

18. (D)

19. (B)

Required no. of screws $= 6097 \times 30 = 182910$

20. (D)

Required value $= 10000000 - 7346879$
$$= 2653121$$

21. (C)

Required mass = 14.250 × 19 = 270.75 kg

22. (B)

Greater number = 9470587 + 6976583

   = 16447170

23. (B)

24. (C)

Required number = 3760924 + 39067

   = 3799991

25. (B)

Cost of 479 chairs = 1479 × 479 = 708441

HOTS (ACHIEVERS SECTION)

26. (B)	27. (A)	28. (C)	29. (B)	30. (C)

26. (B)

Distance = Speed × Time = 65× 25 = 1625 km

27. (A)

Largest 3-digit number = 999

Smallest 3-digit number = 100

Sum = 999 + 100 = 1099

Difference = 999 – 100 = 899

Product = 1099 × 899 = 988001

28. (C)

$$\frac{\text{Defective bulbs}}{\text{Total bulbs}} = \frac{2}{10} = \frac{x}{820}$$

$$x = \frac{2 \times 820}{10} = 164$$

29. (B)

$$\text{Circumference} = \pi d = \frac{22}{7} \times 70 = 220 \ cm$$

$$\text{Number of revolution} = \frac{1.65 \times 1000 \times 100}{220}$$

$$= \frac{165 \times 1000}{220} = 750$$

30. (C)

$$\frac{234 \times 20}{15} = 312 \ kg$$

2. PLAYING WITH NUMBERS

Answer Key

1. (C)	2. (B)	3. (D)	4. (D)	5. (B)	6. (D)	7. (C)	8. (B)	9. (D)	10. (B)
11. (A)	12. (C)	13. (D)	14. (B)	15. (B)	16. (B)	17. (D)	18. (D)	19. (A)	20. (D)
21. (A)	22. (A)	23. (A)	24. (C)	25. (B)					

1. (C)

$$\begin{array}{ccc} 76 & 113 & 186 \\ -4 & -5 & -6 \\ \hline 72 & 108 & 180 \end{array}$$

HCF of 72 and 108 = 36

HCF of 108 and 180 = 36

∴ required number = 36

2. (B)

LCM of 16, 36 and 40 is

$$\begin{array}{c|ccc} 2 & 16, & 36, & 40 \\ 2 & 8, & 18, & 20 \\ 2 & 4, & 9, & 10 \\ \hline & 2, & 9, & 5 \end{array}$$

∴ LCM = 2 × 2 × 2 × 2 × 9 × 5

   = 16 × 45 = 720

∴ required number = (720 + 7) = 727

3. (D)

The greatest 4 digit number = 9999.

Here,

2	12, 16, 28, 36
2	6, 8, 14, 18
2	3, 4, 7, 9
3	3, 2, 7, 9
	1, 2, 7, 3

LCM of 12, 16, 28 and 36

$$= 2 \times 2 \times 2 \times 3 \times 2 \times 7 \times 3$$

$$= 4 \times 9 \times 4 \times 7$$

$$= 16 \times 9 \times 7$$

$$= 1008$$

∵ 9072 is a multiple of 1008.

∴ it is the greatest number of 4 digits which is divisible by 12, 16, 28 & 36.

4. (D)

LCM × HCF = one number × second number

$$\Rightarrow \text{Second number} = \frac{23 \times 1449}{161}$$

$$= 23 \times 9$$

$$= 207$$

5. (B)

LCM of 21, 28, 36 and 45 is

3	21, 28, 36, 45
2	7, 28, 12, 15
3	7, 14, 6, 15
2	7, 14, 2, 5
7	7, 7, 1, 5
	1, 1, 1, 5

∴ LCM of 21, 28, 36 and 45

$$= 3 \times 2 \times 3 \times 2 \times 7 \times 5$$

$$= 36 \times 35$$

$$= 1260$$

∴ Required number = 1260 + 3 = 1263

6. (D)

$$\text{Required number} = \frac{\text{HCF} \times \text{LCM}}{\text{one of the numbers}}$$

$$= \frac{145 \times 2175}{725}$$

$$= 435$$

7. (C)

∵ 32 has 1, 2, 4, 8, 16, 32, as its factors.

∴ 32 is a composite number.

8. (B)

Required length = HCF of 700, 385 and 1295

$$= 35 \text{cm}$$

9. (D)

445	572	699
− 4	− 5	− 6
441	567	693

3	441		3	567		3	693
3	147		3	189		3	231
7	49		3	63		7	77
	7		3	21			11
				7			

HCF of 441, 567 and 693 = 3 × 3 × 7

$$= 63$$

∴ Required number = 63

10. (B)

HCF of 1152 and 1664   LCM of 1152, 1664

2	1152,	1664
2	576,	832
2	288	416
2	144	208
2	72	104
2	36	52
2	18	26
	9	13

∴ HCF of 1152 and 1664 = 2^7 = 128

LCM of 1152 and 1664 = $2^7 \times 9 \times 13$ = 14976

∴ LCM + HCF = 14976 + 128 = 15104

11. (A)

$$\text{Required number} = \frac{21 \times 3003}{231}$$

$$= 273$$

12. **(C)**

LCM of 8, 10 and 12

2	8, 10, 12
2	4, 5, 6
	2, 5, 3

∴ LCM of 8, 10, 12 = 2 × 2 × 2 × 5 × 3
$$= 120$$

∴ Greatest 3-digit number which is divisible by 8, 10 and 12 = 120 × 8 = 960

13. **(D)**

$3 + 8 + 7 + 4 + 5 + 9 = 36$

$9 + 0 + 4 + 8 + 0 + 6 = 27$

$7 + 5 + 8 + 9 + 3 + 4 = 36$

$8 + 7 + 9 + 1 + 3 + 4 = 32$

∵ 32 is not divisible by 9.

∴ 879134 is not divisible by 9.

14. **(B)**

LCM of 28, 36 and 45

2	28, 36, 45
2	14, 18, 45
3	7, 9, 45
3	7, 3, 15
	7, 1, 5

∴ LCM of 28, 36 and 45
$$= 2 \times 2 \times 3 \times 3 \times 7 \times 5$$
$$= 4 \times 9 \times 35$$
$$= 140 \times 9$$
$$= 1260$$

∴ Required number = 1260 − 19
$$= 1241$$

15. **(B)**

LCM of 4, 7, 12 and 84 =

2	4, 7, 12, 84
2	2, 7, 6, 42
3	1, 7, 3, 21
7	1, 7, 1, 7
	1, 1, 1, 1

$= 2 \times 2 \times 3 \times 7 = 84$ seconds.

∴ The bells will toll together after 84 seconds.

∴ Number of times the bells will toll together in

28 minutes $= \dfrac{28 \times 60}{84} = 20$

16. **(B)**

LCM of 20, 25, 30 is

2	20, 25, 30
5	10, 25, 15
	2, 5, 3

∴ LCM of 20, 25, 30 = 2 × 5 × 2 × 5 × 3
$$= 300$$

∴ least 5-digit number which is exactly divisible by 20, 25, 30 = 10200.

17. **(D)**

Multiples of 25 between 500 and 700 = 525, 550, 575, 600, 625, 650, 675.

∴ Required number = 650

18. **(D)**

694728 is divisible by 2 as well as 4.

∴ 694728 is divisible by 8.

19. **(A)**

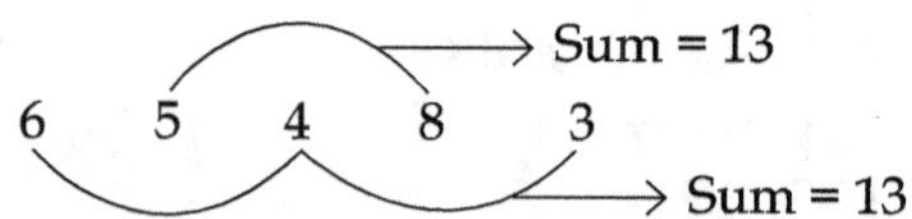

Difference = 13 − 13 = 0

∴ 65483 is divisible by 11.

20. **(D)**

Sum of first five multiples of 23 = 23 + 23 × 2 + 23 × 3 + 23 × 4 + 23 × 5

$= 23 (1 + 2 + 3 + 4 + 5)$

$= 23 \times 15$

$= 345$

21. **(A)**

1509344 is divisible by 8.

22. (A)

467 * 381

The sum of digits of the above number

$$= 4 + 6 + 7 + * + 3 + 8 + 1$$

$$= 10 + 7 + * + 3 + 8 + 1$$

$$= 29 + *$$

If, $* = 1$, then, the sum of digits will become 30.

$\therefore$ required number $= 1$

23. (A)

$1870 + 22 = 1892$

$1870 - 22 = 1848$

24. (C)

Required capacity of bag

= HCF of 120, 144 and 204

= 12 kg

25. (B)

Required time = LCM of 6, 8, 12 and 20

2	6, 8, 12, 20
2	3, 4, 6, 10
3	3, 2, 3, 5
	1, 2, 1, 5

$\therefore$ Required time $= 2 \times 2 \times 3 \times 2 \times 5$

$$= 120 \text{ minutes} = 2 \text{ hr.}$$

$\therefore$ bells will again ring together at $(7 + 2)$

$$= 9 \text{ a.m.}$$

HOTS (ACHIEVERS SECTION)

26. (C)	27. (A)	28. (C)	29. (C)	30. (A)

26. (C)

LCM of 21, 28, 36, 45 = 1260

Required Number = 1260 + 7 = 1267

27. (A)

Sum = 101 + 103 + 107 + 109 + 111 = 531

28. (C)

$285 - 9 = 276$; $1249 - 7 = 1242$

HCF of 276 and 1242 = 138

29. (C)

LCM of 2, 3, 7, 12, 16, 18, 30 = 5040

30. (A)

Let the number be x

$3x - 5 = 16$

$$3x = 21 \Rightarrow x = \frac{21}{3} = 7$$

3. BASIC GEOMETRICAL IDEAS

Answer Key

1. (A)	2. (A)	3. (A)	4. (C)	5. (A)	6. (B)	7. (B)	8. (C)	9. (D)	10. (A)
11. (B)	12. (C)	13. (C)	14. (D)	15. (B)	16. (B)	17. (B)	18. (D)	19. (A)	20. (B)

1. (A)

The polygon of n sides = $n(n - 3)/2$

Hexagon has 6 sides = $6(6 - 3)/2 = 9$

5. (A)

Find r

The distance from the center point to any point on the circle is called the radius of a circle. Here, r is the radius in the figure. Hence, the correct answer is option A.

9. (D)

A chord divides a circle into two segments.

11. (B)

A plane figure can be made of straight lines,

curved lines, or both straight and curved lines. Triangle is a plane figure which is made up of three line segments or sides.Hence, B will be correct answer.

12. (C)
A plane figure can be made of straight lines, curved lines, or both straight and curved lines. Pentagon is a plane figure which is made up of five line segments. Hence, C will be correct answer.

13. (C)
The common initial point is known as vertex of the angle. Hence, it lies on the angle.

14. (D)
Possible angle form by given figure are ∠AOB, ∠AOC, ∠AOD, ∠BOC, ∠BOD, ∠COD.
So, there are 6 total angles formed
Hence, option D is correct.

15. (B)
∠XYZ can be written as ∠XYP, ∠XYZ, ∠Y, ∠ZYX, ∠PYX
They all represent same angle with different naming style.
But, ∠ZXY does not represent this angle, it is other angle because there is X in center of this angle.
So, option B is correct.

16. (B)
Given,
Number of points = 5
We know that
Number of line segments $= \{n \times (n-1)\}/2$
where n = number of points.
Therefore Number of line segments in the given line= $\{5 \times (5 - 1)\}/2 = 10$

17. (B)
Given,
Number of sides in the polygon = sum of the two least consecutive primes
$= 2 + 3$ (because 2 and 3 are least consecutive prime number) $= 5$
We know that
The number of diagonal $= \{n(n-3)\}/2$ where, n= no. of sides
$= \{ 5 (5-3) \} /2 = 5$

19. (A)
A polygon is a simple closed curve made up of line segments. Hence, option A is correct.

20. (B)
Option B is right
For a regular polygon, all sides and all angle must be equal to each other.
And the only figure (ii) follows this condition.

HOTS (ACHIEVERS SECTION)

21. (A)	22. (A)	23. (B)	24. (B)	25. (D)

21. (A)
(a) The given curve is an open curve
(b) The given curve is a closed curve
(c) The given curve is a closed curve
(d) The given curve is a closed curve

22. (A)
The angles are ∠DAB, ∠ABC, ∠BCD and ∠CDA

23. (B)
∠ABD and ∠ABC are triangles which have ∠B as common.

25. (D)

Option A is true as each diagonal of a quadrilateral divides it into two triangles.

Option B is also correct as it is not possible to construct a quadrilateral with one side greater than the sum of three other sides.

Option C is also true as a quadrilateral can at most have three obtuse angles. All the four angles cannot be obtuse and sum of 4 angles of a quadrilateral is 360°.

Option D is incorrect. A quadrilateral does not have four diagonals.A quadrilateral has exactly two diagonals.So, option (D) is false.

Answer Key

1. (B)	2. (B)	3. (A)	4. (C)	5. (A)	6. (B)	7. (A)	8. (A)	9. (A)	10. (B)
11. (C)	12. (A)	13. (C)	14. (C)	15. (D)	16. (A)	17. (C)	18. (A)	19. (B)	20. (A)

HOTS (ACHIEVERS SECTION)

21. (B)	22. (C)	23. (A)	24. (C)	25. (D)

21. (B)

For a regular polygon, all sides and all angle must be equal to each other. And, only figure (ii) follows this condition.

22. (C)

If one angle is right angle then the other both angles are a complementary angle in a triangle.

23. (A)

A polygon is a simple closed curve made up of line segments. Hence, option A is correct.

24. (C)

For any polyhedron, Euler's formula ;

$F + V - E = 2$

Where, F = Face and V = Vertices and E = Edges

Given, $F = V = 5$

On putting the values of F and V in the about formulae,

$5 + 5 - E = 2$

$10 - E = 2$

$E = 8$

5. INTEGERS

Answer Key

1. (A)	2. (C)	3. (A)	4. (B)	5. (A)	6. (A)	7. (B)	8. (A)	9. (B)	10. (B)
11. (A)	12. (A)	13. (A)	14. (C)	15. (D)	16. (A)	17. (B)	18. (A)	19. (C)	20. (D)
21. (A)	22. (B)	23. (B)	24. (B)	25. (C)					

1. (A)

$? = 9(-16) + (-12)\,(-16)$

$= -144 + 192 = 48$

2. (C)

$? = (-12)7 + (-12)\,(-4)$

$= -84 + 48 = -36$

3. (A)

$-47 + x = 65$

$\Rightarrow x = 65 + 47 = 112$

4. (B)

$32 - x = -27$

$\Rightarrow x = 32 + 27 = 59$

5. (A)

Required result $= [33 + (-47)] - (-84)$

$= -14 + 84 = 70$

6. (A)

$? = [37 - (-6)] + [11 - (-32)]$

$= (37 + 6) + (11 + 32) = 43 + 43 = 86$

7. (B)

$265 + x = -27$

$\Rightarrow x = -27 - 265 = -292$

8. **(A)**
$37 - (-1070 + 813)$
$= 37 - (-257) = 37 + 257 = 294$

9. **(B)**
Successor of $-99 = -99 + 1 = -98$

10. **(B)**
Predecessor of $-79 = -79 - 1 = -80$

11. **(A)**
Required sum $= (-23) + 62 + (-57) + 13$
$= -23 + 62 - 57 + 13$
$= -80 + 75 = -5$

12. **(A)**

13. **(A)**
$5 - 2 - 7 + 6 = 11 - 9 = 2$

14. **(C)**
$-2 - 7 + 3 + 6 - 9 + 11$
$= -18 + 20 = 2$

15. **(D)**
Required result $= -7 - (-5 + 12)$
$= -7 - 7 = -14$

16. **(A)**
Net balance $= 28760 - 12380 = ₹\ 16380$

17. **(B)**
$\left|-5 - 26 + 17\right| = \left|-31 + 17\right| = \left|-14\right| = 14$

18. **(A)**
$57 + x = -79 \Rightarrow x = -79 - 57 = -136$

19. **(C)**
$(7896 - 5396) - (-2473)$
$= 2500 + 2473 = 4973$

20. **(D)**
$-49 + (72 - (-99)]$
$= -49 + (72 + 99)$
$= -49 + 171 = 122$

21. **(A)**
Required value
$= 1701 - 473 - 375 - 383 - 283$
$= 1701 - 1514 = 187$

22. **(B)**
$-173 + x = -307$
$\Rightarrow x = -307 + 173$
$\Rightarrow x = -134$

23. **(B)**
Required value
$= (-705 - 317) + (487 + 265)$
$= -1022 + 752 = -270$

24. **(B)**
Predecessor of $-1709 = -1710$
Successor of $-2305 = -2304$
$\therefore$ Sum of -1710 & $-2304 = -4014$

25. **(C)**
Required difference
$1000 - (-999) = 1000 + 999 = 1999$

HOTS (ACHIEVERS SECTION)				
26. (B)	27. (C)	28. (A)	29. (B)	30. (C)

6. FRACTIONS

Answer Key

1. (C)	2. (A)	3. (D)	4. (A)	5. (B)	6. (C)	7. (C)	8. (B)	9. (D)	10. (B)
11. (C)	12. (B)	13. (D)	14. (B)	15. (C)	16. (D)	17. (A)	18. (B)	19. (A)	20. (A)
21. (B)	22. (B)	23. (B)	24. (B)	25. (C)					

1. (C)

2. (A)

   Required value

   $$= 19 - \frac{29}{3} = \frac{57-29}{3} = \frac{28}{3} = 9\frac{1}{3}$$

3. (D)

4. (A)

   Required amount of milk

   $$= \frac{15}{2} - \frac{23}{4} = \frac{30-23}{4} = \frac{7}{4} = 1\frac{3}{4} \text{ litre}$$

5. (B)

   $$6\frac{1}{2} - 5\frac{2}{3} + 3\frac{1}{4}$$

   $$= \frac{13}{2} - \frac{17}{3} + \frac{13}{4} = \frac{78-68+39}{12}$$

   $$= \frac{49}{12} = 48\frac{1}{12} = \frac{49}{12} = 48\frac{1}{12}$$

6. (C)

   Required value =

   $$5 - \frac{2}{3} - \frac{3}{4} = \frac{60-8-9}{12} = \frac{60-17}{12}$$

   $$= \frac{43}{12} = 3\frac{7}{12}$$

7. (C)

   Required value $= \frac{7}{8} - \frac{5}{12} = \frac{21-10}{24} = \frac{11}{24}$

8. (B)

   Required value =

   $$8 - \frac{11}{6} = \frac{48-11}{6} = \frac{37}{6} = 6\frac{1}{6}$$

9. (D)

   $$\frac{3}{5} = \frac{3 \times 7}{5 \times 7} = \frac{21}{35}$$

10. (B)

    $$\frac{5}{12} = \frac{5 \times 7}{12 \times 7} = \frac{35}{84}$$

11. (C)

    $$\frac{56}{70} = \frac{4}{5}$$

12. (B)

    $$\frac{4}{5} > \frac{2}{3} \Rightarrow 12 > 10$$

13. (D)

    $$\frac{2}{5} > \frac{1}{3} \Rightarrow 6 > 5$$

    $$\frac{1}{4} > \frac{2}{3} < \frac{1}{4} > \frac{2}{3} \Rightarrow 3 < 8$$

    $$\frac{4}{5} < \frac{6}{7} \Rightarrow 28 < 30$$

    $$\frac{1}{7} > \frac{3}{5} \Rightarrow 5 > 21 \text{ (Not correct)}$$

14. (B)

    Required length =

    $$\frac{15}{4} - \frac{5}{8} = \frac{30-5}{8} = \frac{25}{8} = 3\frac{1}{8}$$

15. (C)

    Here,

    $$40 - \frac{29}{3} = \frac{120-29}{3} = \frac{91}{3} = 30\frac{1}{3}$$

16. (D)

    $$3 + \frac{6}{5} - \frac{7}{3} + \frac{11}{5} = \frac{45+18-35+33}{15}$$

    $$= \frac{61}{15} = 4\frac{1}{15}$$

17. (A)

    $$5 - \frac{1}{2} + \frac{1}{3} - \frac{1}{4} = \frac{60-6+4-3}{12} = \frac{64-9}{12}$$

    $$= \frac{55}{12} = 4\frac{7}{12}$$

18. (B)

    $$7 + \frac{1}{5} - \frac{7}{3} + \frac{9}{2}$$

$$= \frac{210+6-70+135}{30} = \frac{351-70}{30} = \frac{281}{30}$$

$$= 9\frac{11}{30}$$

19. (A)

$$\frac{6}{5} < \frac{3}{2} < \frac{8}{5} < \frac{7}{4}$$

20. (A)

$$\frac{17}{2} - \frac{20}{3} = \frac{51-40}{6} = \frac{11}{6} = 1\frac{5}{6}$$

21. (B)

$$5 - \frac{17}{5} = \frac{25-17}{5} = \frac{8}{5} = 1\frac{3}{5}$$

22. (B)

$$8\frac{1}{3} - 7\frac{2}{5} + 4\frac{2}{3} - 6\frac{1}{5}$$

$$= \frac{25}{3} - \frac{37}{5} + \frac{14}{3} - \frac{31}{5}$$

$$= \frac{125-111+70-93}{15}$$

$$= \frac{195-204}{15}$$

$$= \frac{-9}{15} = \frac{-3}{5}$$

23. (B)

Required expression

$$= 14 - [12 - \{9 - (7 - 6 - 2)\}]$$

$$= 14 - [12 - \{9 - (7 - 4)\}]$$
$$= 14 - [12 - \{9 - 3\}]$$
$$= 14 - [12 - 6]$$
$$= 14 - 6 = 8$$

24. (B) Given expression

$$= \left[\frac{36}{7} - \left\{ \frac{33}{10} + \left(\frac{14}{5} - \frac{7}{10} \right) \right\} \right]$$

$$= \left[\frac{36}{7} - \left\{ \frac{33}{10} + \left(\frac{28-7}{10} \right) \right\} \right]$$

$$= \left[\frac{36}{7} - \left\{ \frac{33}{10} + \frac{21}{10} \right\} \right]$$

$$= \frac{36}{7} - \frac{54}{10}$$

$$= \frac{360-378}{70} = \frac{-18}{70} = \frac{-9}{35}$$

25. (C)

$$\frac{3}{4} of \left(\frac{2}{3} - \frac{2}{5} \right) + \frac{1}{2} \div \frac{5}{2}$$

$$= \frac{3}{4} of \left(\frac{10-6}{15} \right) + \frac{1}{2} \div \frac{5}{2}$$

$$= \frac{3}{4} of \frac{4}{15} + \frac{1}{2} \div \frac{5}{2}$$

$$= \frac{1}{5} + \frac{1}{2} \times \frac{2}{5}$$

$$= \frac{1}{5} + \frac{1}{5} = \frac{2}{5}$$

HOTS (ACHIEVERS SECTION)

26. (A)	27. (C)	28. (B)	29. (B)	30. (B)

26. (A)

$$\text{Required fraction} = \frac{12\,\text{minutes}}{60\,\text{minutes}} = \frac{1}{5}$$

27. (C)

$$\frac{P-3}{2} - 5 = \frac{P-1}{3} + 7$$

$$\frac{P-3-10}{2} = \frac{P-1+21}{3}$$

$$\frac{P-13}{2} = \frac{P+20}{3}$$

$$3P - 39 = 2P + 40$$

$3P - 2P = 40 + 39$

$P = 79$

28. **(B)**

$$5\frac{1}{2} - 3\frac{2}{3} + 7\frac{1}{5} - 6\frac{1}{4}$$

$$\frac{11}{2} - \frac{11}{3} + \frac{36}{5} - \frac{25}{4} = \frac{330 - 220 + 432 - 375}{60}$$

$$= \frac{762 - 595}{60} = \frac{167}{60} = 2\frac{47}{60}$$

29. **(B)**

LCM of 7, 3, 8, 6, 9 = 504

$$\frac{4}{7} = \frac{4 \times 72}{7 \times 72} = \frac{288}{504} ; \frac{2}{3} = \frac{2 \times 168}{3 \times 168} = \frac{336}{504}$$

$$\frac{1}{8} = \frac{1 \times 63}{8 \times 63} = \frac{63}{504} ; \frac{5}{6} = \frac{5 \times 84}{6 \times 84} = \frac{420}{504}$$

$$\frac{7}{9} = \frac{7 \times 56}{9 \times 56} = \frac{392}{504}$$

$\frac{5}{6}$ is the largest

30. **(B)**

7. DECIMALS

Answer Key

1. (A)	2. (B)	3. (A)	4. (B)	5. (C)	6. (B)	7. (C)	8. (A)	9. (B)	10. (B)
11. (C)	12. (A)	13. (B)	14. (D)	15. (B)	16. (A)	17. (C)	18. (C)	19. (A)	20. (D)
21. (B)	22. (C)	23. (C)	24. (D)	25. (C)					

1. **(A)**
   Given expression can be written as
   $8 + 0.3 + 0.04 + 0.007 = 8.347$

2. **(B)**
   We have $7\frac{1}{25} = 7 + \frac{1}{25} = 7.04$

3. **(A)**
   $6 - 0.23 + 1.2 - 5.76$
   $= 7.2 - 5.99 = 1.21$

4. **(B)**
   $37 - 35.79 = 1.21$

5. **(C)**
   Required number $= 81 - 74.5 = 6.5$

6. **(B)**
   Required number $= 7.3 - 0.867 = 6.433$

7. **(C)**
   Required number $= 79.5 - 27.89 = 51.61$

8. **(A)**
   Required number $= 53 - 32.754 = 20.246$

9. **(B)**
   $76.3 - 7.666 - 6.77 - 5.55$
   $= 76.3 - 19.986 = 56.314$

10. **(B)**
    Here, 37 mm $= \frac{37}{10} = 3.7$ cm

    and 37 cm $= \frac{3.7}{100} = 0.037$ m

11. **(C)**
    2 kg 57 g $= 2 \times 1000 + 57 = 2057$ g

    and $\frac{2057}{1000} = 2.057$ kg

12. **(A)**
    Total earning $= 302.80 + 379.20 + 297.60$
    $= 979.60$

13. **(B)**
    We have $15\frac{17}{40} = 15 + \frac{17}{40}$

$$= 15 + 0.425$$
$$= 15.425$$

14. (D)

Here, 5kg 75g + 3kg 465g = 8kg 540g

∴ 9kg – 8kg 540g = 460g

15. (B)

Here, 4.902 + 15.376 = 20.278

then 20.278 – 16.307 = 3.971

16. (A)

7kg 207g – 6kg 40g = 1kg 167g

17. (C)

18. (C)

19. (A)

Total length of cloth = 2m 5cm + 3m 35cm
$$= 5m\ 40cm$$

20. (D)

Required distance

$$= 17 - (9km\ 65m + 4km\ 75m)$$
$$= 17 - (13\ km\ 140\ m)$$
$$= 3km\ 860m$$

21. (B)

Required number = 73 – 29.13 = 43.87

22. (C)

Required balance = 1000 – 447.85 = ₹ 552.15

23. (C)

Cost of fooding

$$= 2000 - (439.75 + 208.75 + 524.25)$$
$$= 2000 - 1172.75$$
$$= 827.25$$

HOTS (ACHIEVERS SECTION)

26. (D)	27. (B)	28. (B)	29. (C)	30. (B)

26. (D)

$$\text{Required distance} = \frac{111 \times 15}{6} = 277.5\ km$$

27. (B)

$$1 + 0.1 + 0.01 + 0.001 = 1.111$$

28. (B)

$$0.213 \div 0.00213$$

$$= \frac{213}{1000} \div \frac{213}{100000} = \frac{213}{1000} \times \frac{100000}{213} = 100$$

29. (C)

$$\frac{144}{0.144} = \frac{14.4}{x}$$

$$x = \frac{0.144 \times 14.4}{144} = \frac{144 \times 144}{144 \times 1000 \times 10}$$

$$= \frac{144}{10000} = 0.0144$$

30. (B)

8. DATA HANDLING

Answer Key

1. (C)	2. (C)	3. (A)	4. (D)	5. (A)	6. (A)	7. (C)	8. (B)	9. (A)	10. (A)
11. (A)	12. (B)	13. (D)	14. (B)	15. (C)	16. (B)	17. (B)	18. (A)	19. (A)	20. (A)

6. (A)

According to the graph,

The number of subscribers in region M is 3000.

The number of subscribers in region N is 4000.

The number of subscribers in region O is 1000.

The number of subscribers in region P is 2000.

We can see that number of subscribers in combined region of regions M and N is 3000 + 4000 = 7000

We can see that number of subscribers in combined region of regions M , N, O, P is 3000 + 4000 + 1000 + 2000 =10000.

Therefore Region M + Region N subscribers = 70 percent of total subscribers.

So, the correct option is A.

11. (A)

The given bar graph represents the number of matches played by cricket teams of different country.

We can prepare frequency table from given bar graph as follows:

Country	No. of matches
India	30
Pakistan	24
West Indies	20
England	28
South Africa	18
Australia	32
Sri Lanka	24

Total number of students = 176

Then, the number of more matches played by India than Pakistan

= Number of matches played by India − Number of matches played by Pakistan

= 30 − 24 = 6 matches.

That is, India played 6 matches more than Pakistan.

Hence, option A is correct.

12. (B)

Saturday = 4 × 2= 8

Wednesday = 6 × 2 = 12

Therefore required ratio is 8 : 12 = 2 : 3

13. (D)

The given bar graph represents the number of matches played by cricket teams of different country.

We can prepare frequency table from given bar graph as follows:

Country	No. of matches
India	30
Pakistan	24
West Indies	20
England	28
South Africa	18
Australia	32
Sri Lanka	24

Total number of students = 176

The country that played maximum number of matches will have the highest number of matches.

Clearly, the maximum number of matches are played by Australia (32).

Hence, option D is correct.

14. (B)

From given pictograph, we can find the number of ice cream cons sold during a week as following:

Monday = 10

Tuesday = 16

Wednesday = 12

Thursday = 7

Friday = 14

Saturday = 8

Therefore total number of ice cream = 67

15. (C)

Number of ice creams sold on friday

= 7 × 2 = 14

therefore sale value on Thursday

= Rs. 20 × 14

= Rs. 280

16. (B)

The given bar graph represents the number of matches played by cricket teams of different country.

We can prepare frequency table from given bar graph as follows:

Country	No. of matches
India	30
Pakistan	24

West Indies	20
England	28
South Africa	18
Australia	32
Sri Lanka	24

Total number of students = 176

Then, the ratio of number of matches played by India to the number of matches played by Sri Lanka

$$= \frac{30}{24} = \frac{5}{4} = 5:4$$

Hence, the required ratio is 5:4.

Therefore, option B is correct.

HOTS (ACHIEVERS SECTION)

21. (D)	22. (A)	23. (B)	24. (D)	25. (D)

21. **(D)**

Number of wall clocks sold on Tuesday

$= 5 \times 5 = 25$

Number of wall clocks sold on Thursday

$= 5 \times 7 = 35$

Therefore required difference $= 35 \times 25 = 10$

23. **(B)**

The letter k is used to denote 1000

Therefore, Number of traffic accidents in the year 2001 = 260k

$= 260 \times 1000$

$= 260,000$

Number of traffic accidents in year 2004

$= 220k$

$= 220 \times 1000$

$= 220,000$

Then, the difference $= 260,000 \times 220,000$

$= 40,000$

Therefore, option B is correct.

24. **(D)**

As shown in the figure, the sale was maximum on Thursday. Hence the correct answer is option D.

25. **(D)**

If we study the given pictograph carefully, we can see that one ball represents 17 students.

Against dart board, we can see 8 balls.

So, the number of students who participated in dart board $= 17 \times 8 = 136$

Hence, 136 students tried the dart board.

9. MENSURATION

Answer Key

1. (C)	2. (D)	3. (B)	4. (A)	5. (C)	6. (B)	7. (B)	8. (C)	9. (A)	10. (C)
11. (B)	12. (B)	13. (C)	14. (A)	15. (C)	16. (B)	17. (B)	18. (C)	19. (A)	20. (D)
21. (D)	22. (B)	23. (B)	24. (B)	25. (B)					

1. **(C)**

If x is required length then

$x + x + x = 267$

$3x = 267 \Rightarrow x = \dfrac{267}{3} = 89$ cm

2. **(D)**

Here, 3 × perimeter of rectangular ground

$= 7800$ m

$\Rightarrow 3 [2 (l + b)] = 7800$

$$\Rightarrow l + 330 = \dfrac{7800}{6}$$

$$\Rightarrow l + 330 = 1300$$

$$\Rightarrow l = 1300 - 330 = 970 \text{ m}$$

3. **(B)**

Perimeter of isosceles triangle

$= 8.5 + 8.5 + 7 = 24$ cm

4. **(A)**

Perimeter of regular hexagon

$= 6 \times 6.5$ cm $= 39$ cm

5. **(C)**

Here, Perimeter $= \dfrac{1980}{18} = 110$ m

If l and b are its length and breadth, then

$$\Rightarrow 2\,(l + b) = 110$$

$$\Rightarrow 2\,(l + 23) = 110$$

$$\Rightarrow l + 23 = 55 \Rightarrow l = 55 - 23 = 32 \text{ m}$$

6. **(B)**

Circumference of circle $= 66$

$2\pi r = 66$ where r is radius

$$\therefore 2r = \dfrac{66}{\pi} = \dfrac{66}{\dfrac{22}{7}} = \dfrac{66 \times 7}{22} = 21 \text{ cm}$$

7. **(B)**

Given,

$2\pi r = 264$ where r is radius

$$\therefore r = \dfrac{264}{2 \times \pi} = \dfrac{264 \times 7}{2 \times 22} = 42 \text{ cm}$$

8. **(C)**

Circumference of wheel of car

$$= 2\pi r = 2 \times \dfrac{22}{7} \times \dfrac{70}{2} = 220 \text{ m}$$

$$\therefore \text{Required no. of revolutions} = \dfrac{1650}{220}$$

$$= 7\dfrac{1}{2}$$

9. **(A)**

Circumference of circle

$$2\pi r = \dfrac{22}{7} \times 35 = 22 \times 5 = 110 \text{ cm}$$

10. **(C)**

If b is breadth of rectangle then

$$35 \times b = 630 \Rightarrow b = \dfrac{630}{35} = 18 \text{ cm}$$

Perimeter $= 2\,(l + b) = 2\,(35 + 18)$

$$= 2 \times 53 = 106 \text{ cm}$$

11. **(B)**

Area of the room $= \dfrac{5100}{85} = 60 \text{ m}^2$

If b is its width then

$l \times b = 60$

$$8 \times b = 60 \Rightarrow b = \dfrac{60}{8} = 7.5 \text{ m}$$

12. **(B)**

Breadth of rectangle

$$b = \dfrac{540}{36} = 15 \text{ cm}$$

$\therefore$ Perimeter of rectangle $= 2\,(36 + 15)$

$$= 2 \times 51 = 102 \text{ cm.}$$

13. **(C)**

Area of square $= \dfrac{1}{2} \times \left(5\sqrt{2}\right)^2$

$$= \dfrac{1}{2} \times 25 \times 2$$

$$= 25 \text{ cm}^2$$

14. **(A)**

If $5x$ and $3x$ are length and breadth then

$2\,(5x + 3x) = 128$

$$\Rightarrow x = \dfrac{128}{16} = 8$$

$\therefore\ l = 5 \times 8 = 40$ m

and $b = 3 \times 8 = 24$ m

Hence, area $= l \times b = 40 \times 24 = 960 \text{ m}^2$

15. **(C)**

Required no. of square tiles

$$= \frac{12 \times 100 \times 8 \times 100}{10 \times 10}$$

$$= 9600$$

16. **(B)**
Area of one flower bed = 3 × 3
$$= 9 \text{ cm}^2$$
Area of five flower beds = 9 × 5 = 45 cm^2
Area of rectangular field = 17 × 5
$$= 85 \text{ cm}^2$$
Area of remaining part = 85 − 45
$$= 40 \text{ cm}^2$$

17. **(B)**
Missing value = 37 − (5 + 4 + 17)
$$= 37 - 26 = 11 \text{ cm}$$

18. **(C)**
Area of square = 2401 = 49 × 49
∴ Side of square = 49 cm
Hence, perimeter of square
= 4 × side = 4 × 49 = 196 cm

19. **(A)**

Area of square $= \dfrac{1}{2} \times (\text{diagonal})^2$

$$= \frac{1}{2} \times \left(8\sqrt{2}\right)^2$$

$$= \frac{1}{2} \times 64 \times 2$$

$$= 64 \text{ cm}^2$$

∴ Side of square = 8 cm
Hence, perimeter of square
$$= 4 \times 8 = 32 \text{ cm}$$

20. **(D)**
Area of floor = 7 × 5 = 35 m^2

Area of carpet = 4 × 4 = 16 m^2
Remaining part = 35 − 16 = 19 m^2

21. **(D)**

Area of floor $= 7 \times 4\dfrac{25}{100}$

$$= 7 \times 4\frac{1}{4}$$

$$= 7 \times \frac{17}{4}$$

$$= 29.75 \text{ m}^2$$

22. **(B)**
Required no. of square tiles

$$= \frac{9 \times 100 \times 6 \times 100}{15 \times 15}$$

$$= 3 \times 2 \times 20 \times 20$$

$$= 2400$$

23. **(B)**
Given, Area of rectangle = area of square
$$\Rightarrow l \times 12 = (18)^2$$

$$\Rightarrow l = \frac{18 \times 18}{12} = 27 \text{ m}$$

24. **(B)**

Cost of tiling $= \dfrac{400 \times 100}{7} = \dfrac{40000}{7}$

$$= ₹ \, 5714.285$$

25. **(B)**
Perimeter = 2 (l + b)
New perimeter = 2 (2l + 2b)
$$= 2 \times 2 \, (l + b)$$
$$= 2 \times \text{initial perimeter.}$$

HOTS (ACHIEVERS SECTION)

26. (D)	27. (C)	28. (C)	29. (A)	30. (B)

26. **(D)**

Perimeter of square field $= \dfrac{4480}{35} = 128$

4 × side = 128 ⇒ side = 32 m
Area = (32)^2 = 1024 m^2

Answer Key

1. (B)	2. (B)	3. (D)	4. (B)	5. (B)	6. (A)	7. (D)	8. (A)	9. (C)	10. (C)
11. (B)	12. (B)	13. (D)	14. (B)	15. (A)	16. (A)	17. (B)	18. (C)	19. (D)	20. (C)
21. (B)	22. (B)	23. (D)	24. (A)	25. (C)					

1. (B)

$2x^2 - y^2 + 3z^2$

$= 2(4)^2 - (-1)^2 + 3(-2)^2$

$= 32 - 1 + 12 = 44 - 1 = 43$

2. (B)

$x^3 + 3x^2 - x + 1 - 5x^3 + 2x^2 - 6x - 7$

$= -4x^3 + 5x^2 - 7x - 6$

3. (D)

Required difference

$= 2x - 3y + 4z - (2x + 5y - 6z + 2)$

$= 2x - 3y + 4z - 2x - 5y + 6z + 2$

$= -8y + 10z + 2$

4. (B)

$2x - [3y - \{2x - (y - x)\}]$

$= 2x - [3y - \{2x - y + x)\}]$

$= 2x - [3y - 3x + y] = 2x - 4y + 3x = 5x - 4y$

5. (B)

Given $\dfrac{2m}{3} + 8 = \dfrac{m}{2} - 1$

$\Rightarrow \dfrac{m}{2} - \dfrac{2m}{3} = 8 + 1$.

$\Rightarrow -\dfrac{3m - 4m}{6} = 9$

$\Rightarrow -m = 6 \times 9 \Rightarrow m = -54$

6. (A)

$3(x + 6) + 2(x + 3) = 64$

$\Rightarrow 3x + 18 + 2x + 6 = 64$

$\Rightarrow 5x + 24 = 64$

$\Rightarrow 5x = 64 - 24$

$\Rightarrow 5x = 40$

$\Rightarrow x = \dfrac{40}{5} = 8$

7. (D)

Here, $3(2 - 5p) - 2(1 - 6p) = 1$

$\Rightarrow 6 - 15p - 2 + 12p = 1$

$\Rightarrow 4 - 3p = 1 \Rightarrow 3p = 4 - 1$

$\Rightarrow 3p = 3 \Rightarrow p = \dfrac{3}{3} = 1$

8. (A)

Let the number be x.

$\therefore 3x - 8 = 13 \Rightarrow 3x = 13 + 8$

$\Rightarrow 3x = 21$

$\Rightarrow x = \dfrac{21}{3} = 7$

9. (C)

Let the numbers be $x, x + 1, x + 2$.

$\therefore x + x + 1 + x + 2 = 114$

$\Rightarrow 3x + 3 = 114 \Rightarrow 3x = 114 - 3$

$\Rightarrow 3x = 111 \Rightarrow x = \dfrac{111}{3} = 37$

Greatest number $= 37 + 2 = 39$

10. (C)

Let the breadth be x m.

Length $= (x + 5)$

Perimeter of rectangle $= 74$

$\Rightarrow 2(x + 5 + x) = 74$

$\Rightarrow 2x + 5 = 37 \Rightarrow 2x = 37 - 5$

$\Rightarrow 2x = 32$

$\Rightarrow x = \dfrac{32}{2} = 16$ m

Length $= 16 + 5 = 21$ m

11. (B)

Let the number be x.

$2x + 9 = 57 \Rightarrow 2x = 57 - 9 = 48$

HINTS AND SOLUTIONS

$x = 24$

12. **(B)**

Let the number be x.

$\therefore x - 7 = 37 \Rightarrow x = 37 + 7 = 44$

13. **(D)**

Let the age of daughter be x years.

$\therefore$ Man's age $= 3x$.

and 5 years ago, daughter's age $= x - 5$

$\therefore$ Man's age $= 3x - 5$

$\Rightarrow 3x - 5 = 4x - 20 \Rightarrow 4x - 3x = -5 + 20$

$\Rightarrow x = 15$ years

14. **(B)**

Let the age of Karan be x years.

Father's age $= 3x$ years

After 14 years,

$3x + 14 = 2(x + 14)$

$\Rightarrow 3x + 14 = 2x + 28$

$\Rightarrow x = 28 - 14$

$\Rightarrow x = 14$ years

15. **(A)**

Let the three consecutive even numbers are

$x, x + 2, x + 4$.

$\therefore x + x + 2 + x + 4 = 78$

$\Rightarrow 3x = 78 - 6$

$\Rightarrow 3x = 72$

$\Rightarrow x = \dfrac{72}{3} = 24$

16. **(A)**

Let the price of the ratio be ₹ x.

$\therefore 5x = 170 + 3x$

$\Rightarrow 2x = 170$

$\Rightarrow x = \dfrac{170}{2} = 85$

17. **(B)**

Let the breadth be x m

Length $= 3x$ m

Perimeter of rectangular park $= 168$

$\Rightarrow 2(l + b) = 168$

$\Rightarrow 2(3x + x) = 168$

$\Rightarrow 8x = 168$

$\Rightarrow x = \dfrac{168}{8} = 21$ m

18. **(C)**

Let the number be x.

$\therefore x \times 17 + 4 = 225$

$\Rightarrow 17x = 225 - 4$

$\Rightarrow 17x = 221$

$\Rightarrow x = \dfrac{221}{17} = 13$

19. **(D)**

Required result

$= 3a - 2b + 5c + 2a + 5b - 7c - a - b + c$

$= 4a + 2b - c$

20. **(C)**

21. **(B)**

Required result $=$

$2a - [3b - \{a - 2c + 3b + 4c - 3a + 3b + 6c\}]$

$= 2a - [3b - \{-2a + 6b + 8c\}]$

$= 2a - [3b + 2a - 6b - 8c]$

$= 2a - [2a - 3b - 8c] = 2a - 2a + 3b + 8c$

$= 3b + 8c$

22. **(B)**

$xy - [yz - zx - \{yx - (3y - xz) - (xy - zy)\}]$

$= xy - [yz - zx - \{yx - 3y + xz - xy + zy\}]$

$= xy - [yz - zx - yx + 3y - xz + xy - zy]$

$= xy + 2xz - 3y$

23. **(D)**

Given $\dfrac{x}{8} - \dfrac{1}{2} = \dfrac{x}{6} - 2$

$\Rightarrow \dfrac{x}{8} - \dfrac{x}{6} = \dfrac{1}{2} - 2$

$\Rightarrow \dfrac{3x - 4x}{24} = \dfrac{1 - 4}{2}$

$\Rightarrow \dfrac{-x}{24} = \dfrac{-3}{2} \Rightarrow -2x = -3 \times 24$

$\Rightarrow x = 36$

24. **(A)**

Let the number be x.

$\therefore\ 3 \times x + 7 = 70$

$\Rightarrow 3x = 70 - 7$

$\Rightarrow 3x = 63$

$\Rightarrow x = \dfrac{63}{3} = 21.$

25. **(C)**

Let the breadth be x.

$\therefore$ Length $= x + 7$

Perimeter of wire $= 86$

$\Rightarrow 2(l + b) = 86$

$\Rightarrow l + b = \dfrac{86}{2}$

$\Rightarrow l + b = 43$

$\Rightarrow x + 7 + x = 43$

$\Rightarrow 2x = 43 - 7$

$\Rightarrow 2x = 36$

$\Rightarrow x = 18$

$\therefore$ Length $= x + 7 = 18 + 7 = 25$ cm

HOTS (ACHIEVERS SECTION)

26. (A)	27. (B)	28. (B)	29. (B)	30. (D)

26. **(A)**

$(a^3 - 4a^2 + 7a - 6) - K = a^2 - 5a + 2$

$K = a^3 - 4a^2 + 7a - 6 - a^2 + 5a - 2$

$= a^3 - 5a^2 + 12a - 8$

27. **(B)**

$16(3x - 5) - 10(4x - 8) = 40$

$48x - 80 - 40x + 80 = 40$

$8x = 40 \Rightarrow x = \dfrac{40}{8} = 5$

11. RATIO AND PROPORTION

Answer Key

1. (B)	2. (B)	3. (A)	4. (A)	5. (B)	6. (D)	7. (B)	8. (C)	9. BC)	10. (C)
11. (B)	12. (D)	13. (A)	14. (A)	15. (B)	16. (A)	17. (B)	18. (B)	19. (A)	20. (B)
21. (D)	22. (C)	23. (B)	24. (C)	25. (B)					

1. **(B)**

No. of envelopes $= \dfrac{35}{87.50} \times 315$

$= \dfrac{350 \times 315}{875} = 126$

2. **(B)**

Weight of 65 magazines $= 13$ kg

$\therefore$ Weight of 1 magazine $= \dfrac{13}{65}$ kg

Weight of 80 magazines $= \dfrac{13}{65} \times 80 = 16$ kg

3. **(A)**

Given,

$\dfrac{\text{boys}}{\text{girls}} = \dfrac{9}{5}$

$\therefore$ No. of girls $= \dfrac{5}{9+5} \times 994$

$= \dfrac{5}{14} \times 994 = 5 \times 71$

$$= 355$$

4. **(A)**

   Given,

   $$\frac{\text{length}}{\text{width}} = \frac{5}{3} = \frac{L}{36}$$

   $$L = \frac{5 \times 36}{3} = 60 \text{ cm}$$

5. **(B)**

   Given,

   $$2x + 3x + 5x = 1020$$
   $$\Rightarrow \quad 10x = 1020$$
   $$\Rightarrow \quad x = \frac{1020}{10} = 102$$

   $\therefore$ Share of C $= 5 \times 102 = 510$

6. **(D)**

   $$\text{Amount of M} = \frac{3}{2+3+4} \times 8100$$
   $$= \frac{3}{9} \times 8100$$
   $$= 3 \times 900$$
   $$= ₹\ 2700$$

7. **(B)**

   $$\frac{\text{speed of bus}}{\text{speed of train}} = \frac{183 \div 3}{426 \div 6} = \frac{61}{71}$$

8. **(C)**

   $$\text{Salary of 15 months} = \frac{63000 \times 14}{7}$$
   $$= ₹\ 126000$$

9. **(B)**

   $$\text{Cost of 26 bananas} = \frac{36 \times 26}{12} = ₹\ 78$$

10. **(C)**

    $$\text{Required weight} = \frac{2}{120} \times 720 = 12 \text{kg}$$

11. **(B)**

    $$\text{Required weight} = \frac{72}{8} \times 18 = 162 \text{ kg}$$

12. **(D)**

    $$\text{Cost of 16 oranges} = \frac{168}{24} \times 16 = ₹\ 112$$

13. **(A)**

    If x is first term, then

    $$x : 12 : : 14 : 8$$
    $$\Rightarrow \frac{x}{12} = \frac{14}{8} \Rightarrow x = \frac{14 \times 12}{8} = 21$$

14. **(A)**

    $$\frac{40 \text{ cm}}{1.5 \text{ m}} = \frac{40 \text{ cm}}{150 \text{ cm}} = \frac{4}{15} = 4:15$$

15. **(B)**

    Given,

    $$x : 92 : : 87 : 116$$
    $$\Rightarrow \frac{x}{92} = \frac{87}{116}$$
    $$\Rightarrow \quad x = \frac{92 \times 87}{116} = 69$$

16. **(A)** Given,

    $$9 : x : : x : 49$$
    $$\Rightarrow \frac{9}{x} = \frac{x}{49} \Rightarrow x \times x = 9 \times 49$$
    $$\Rightarrow x^2 = 9 \times 49$$
    $$\Rightarrow x = \sqrt{9 \times 49} = 3 \times 7 = 21$$

17. **(B)**

    Given,

    $$25 : 35 : : 35 : x$$
    $$\Rightarrow \frac{25}{35} = \frac{35}{x} \Rightarrow x = 49$$

18. **(B)**

    Given,

    $$7 : 42 : : x : 72$$
    $$\Rightarrow \frac{7}{42} = \frac{x}{72} \Rightarrow x = \frac{7 \times 72}{42} = 12$$

19. **(A)**

    Given,

OLYMPIAD WORKBOOK (IMO) CLASS— 6

Income = ₹ 15300

Saving = ₹ 1224

Here, Expenditure = 15300 – 1224 = 14076.

$$\frac{\text{Income}}{\text{Expenditure}} = \frac{15300}{14076} = \frac{25}{23} = 25:23$$

20. (B)

Earning = ₹ 16400

Expenditure = ₹ 7400

Saving = 16400 – 7400 = 9000

$$\frac{\text{Saving}}{\text{Earning}} = \frac{9000}{16400} = \frac{90}{164} = \frac{45}{82} = 45:82$$

21. (D)

Given,

$$\frac{\text{Saving}}{\text{Income}} = \frac{1}{7} \Rightarrow \frac{x}{28000} = \frac{1}{7}$$

$$x = \frac{28000}{7} = 4000$$

22. (C)

Here,

$$\frac{15 \text{ minutes}}{2 \text{ hours}} = \frac{15}{2 \times 60} = \frac{1}{8} = 1:8$$

23. (B)

Here,

$$\frac{210 \text{ grams}}{7 \text{ kg}} = \frac{210}{7 \times 1000} = \frac{3}{100} = 3:100$$

24. (C)

Here,

$$\frac{1.2 \text{ km}}{300 \text{ m}} = \frac{1.2 \times 1000}{300} = \frac{12}{3} = 4:1$$

25. (B)

Given

$$\frac{36}{x} = \frac{x}{16} \Rightarrow x^2 = 36 \times 16$$

$$x = \sqrt{36 \times 16} = 6 \times 4 = 24$$

HOTS (ACHIEVERS SECTION)

26. (B)	27. (A)	28. (A)	29. (A)	30. (C)

26. (B)

$$\text{Share of B} = \frac{5}{(3+5+7)} \times 6900$$

$$= 2300$$

27. (A)

Saving = 7 – 5 = 2

$$\frac{2}{7} = \frac{x}{14000} \Rightarrow x = \frac{2 \times 14000}{7} = 4000$$

28. (A)

Diameter of the pencil = 6 × 2 = 12 mm

$$\text{Required ratio} = \frac{12 \, mm}{15 \times 10 \, mm} = \frac{2}{25} = 2:25$$

12. SYMMETRY

Answer Key

1. (A)	2. (C)	3. (A)	4. (D)	5. (B)	6. (A)	7. (B)	8. (D)	9. (B)	10. (A)
11. (C)	12. (B)	13. (A)	14. (D)	15. (D)	16. (C)	17. (D)	18. (C)	19. (D)	20. (C)

1. (A)

Horizontal and vertical lines through its centre.

2. (C)

The number of lines of symmetry in a regular polygon is equal to the number of sides. A regular hexagon has 6 sides and 6 lines of symmetry.

3. **(A)**
The number of lines of symmetry in a regular polygon is equal to the number of sides. A regular pentagon has 5 sides and 5 lines of symmetry.

4. **(D)**
Lines of symmetry of a square include both its diagonals, the vertical line and the horizontal line through its centre.

5. **(B)**
Both diagonals of a rhombus are lines of symmetry.

6. **(A)**
When the two sides meeting at a vertex has the same length, the line through the vertex is the line of symmetry.

7. **(B)**
Explanation: Drawing a vertical line in the middle of the alphabet V creates two parts that are mirror images of each other

8. **(D)**
Explanation: All 3 medians of the triangle are lines of symmetry.

9. **(B)**
Explanation: Alphabet A has a vertical line of symmetry.

10. **(A)**
Explanation: A general parallelogram has no lines of symmetry. Some special ones (rhombus, rectangle, square) have lines of symmetry.

HOTS (ACHIEVERS SECTION)

21. (D)	22. (C)	23. (D)	24. (D)	25. (A)

22. **(C)**
As shown in the above figure, marked three squares must be added to make the given figure symmetric about the line AB.

23. **(D)**

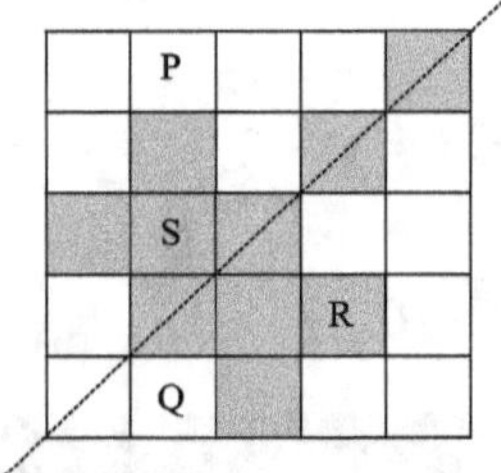

24. **(D)**
All the figures have at least two lines of symmetry.

25. **(A)**
As shown in the figure only one minimum square should be shaded so that the figure has a line of symmetry.

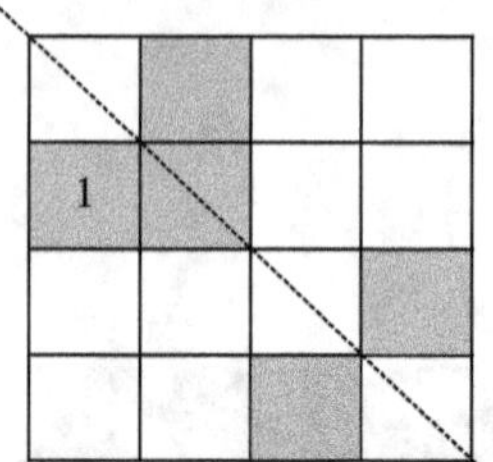

13. GEOMETRY

Answer Key

1. (A)	2. (D)	3. (C)	4. (B)	5. (D)	6. (C)	7. (C)	8. (B)	9. (A)	10. (B)
11. (C)	12. (B)	13. (C)	14. (C)	15. (A)	16. (D)	17. (C)	18. (B)	19. (A)	20. (A)
21. (C)	22. (C)	23. (A)	24. (D)	25. (A)					

OLYMPIAD WORKBOOK (IMO) CLASS— 6

1. **(A)**

   Here,
   $$2x + 3x + 4x = 180°$$
   $$\Rightarrow 9x = 180° \Rightarrow x = \frac{180°}{9} = 20°$$
   Smallest angle $= 2x = 2 \times 20° = 40°$

2. **(B)**

   Vertical angle $= 180° - (65° + 65°)$
   $$= 180° - 130° = 50°$$

3. **(A)**

   Required angle $= \dfrac{360°}{36} = 10°$

4. **(B)**

   Other angle $= 180° - (90° + 55°)$
   $$= 180° - 145° = 35°$$

5. **(A)**

   Here, $\angle A + \angle B + \angle C = 180°$
   $$\Rightarrow 3\angle A = 4\angle B = 6\angle C$$
   $$\Rightarrow \frac{3\angle A}{12} = \frac{4\angle B}{12} = \frac{6\angle C}{12} = x$$
   $$\Rightarrow \angle A = 4x; \ \angle B = 3x; \ \angle C = 2x$$
   $\therefore 4x + 3x + 2x = 180° \Rightarrow 9x = 180° \Rightarrow x = 20°$
   Hence, $\angle A = 4 \times 20° = 80°$

6. **(C)**

   $$3x + 4x + 5x + 6x = 360°$$
   $$\Rightarrow 18x = 360° \Rightarrow x = \frac{360°}{18} = 20°$$
   $\therefore$ Largest angle $= 6 \times 20° = 120°$

HOTS (ACHIEVERS SECTION)

26. (A)	27. (C)	28. (B)	29. (A)	30. (A)

26. **(A)**

   Angle $= \dfrac{360°}{72} = 5°$

27. **(C)**

   Third angle $= 180° - (67° + 43°) = 70°$

28. **(B)**

   $\angle A = 80°$

   $\angle B + \angle C = 180° - 80°$
   $= 100°$

   $\dfrac{1}{2}(\angle B + \angle C) = \dfrac{100°}{2} = 50°;$

   $\angle BOC = 180° - 50° = 130°$

29. **(A)**

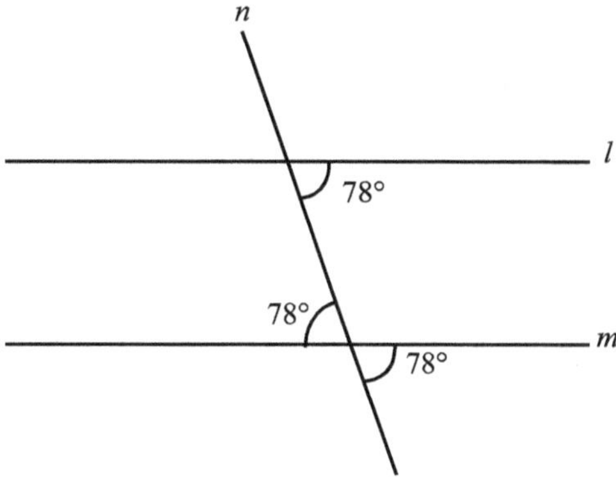

   $x = 78°$ as $l \ // \ m$

14. LOGICAL REASONING

Answer Key

1. (C)	2. (A)	3. (C)	4. (B)	5. (C)	6. (C)	7. (B)	8. (B)	9. (D)	10. (B)
11. (C)	12. (A)	13. (D)	14. (C)	15. (A)	16. (C)	17. (B)	18. (B)	19. (C)	20. (A)
21. (C)	22. (B)	23. (D)	24. (C)	25. (D)	26. (D)	27. (C)	28. (C)	29. (D)	30. (B)
31. (C)	32. (D)	33. (A)	34. (D)	35. (C)	36. (C)	37. (A)	38. (D)	39. (A)	

1. **(C)**
   From figure 1; $(112 \div 14) \times 2 = 16$
   From figure 2; $(168 \div 24) \times 2 = 14$
   From figure 3; $(144 \div 16) \times 2 = 9 \times 2 = 18$

2. **(A)**
   From figure 1; $4 \times 6 + 18 \times 3 = 24 + 54 = 78$
   From figure 2; $3 \times 5 + 24 \times 4 = 15 + 96 = 111$
   From figure 3; $2 \times 7 + 21 \times 4 = 14 + 84 = 98$

3. **(C)**
   $1 + 2 = 3 \to 3^2 = 9$
   $3 + 4 = 7 \to 7^2 = 49$
   $5 + 4 = 9 \to 9^2 = 81$
   $7 + 6 = 13 \to 13^2 = 169$

4. **(B)**
   Physician does the treatment, similarly Judge delivers the judgement.

5. **(C)**
   Effect of Ice is coldness, similarly the effect of Earth is gravitation.

6. **(C)**
   The result of Race is Fatigue, similarly the result of Fast is Hunger.

7. **(B)**
   The given series is

   67   74   81   88   95   102

   $+7 \quad +7 \quad +7 \quad +7 \quad +7$

8. **(B)**
   The given series is

   109   101   94   88   83   79

   $-8 \quad -7 \quad -6 \quad -5 \quad -4$

9. **(D)**
   The given series is

   9   25   49   81   121   169

   $3^2 \quad 5^2 \quad 7^2 \quad 9^2 \quad 11^2 \quad 13^2$

10. **(D)**
    Each letter of the word 'TRUTH' is replaced by a set of two letters – one preceding it and the other following it – in the code. Thus, T is replaced by SU, R is replaced by QS and so on.

11. **(C)**
    All the letters of the word, except the last letter, are written in a reverse order to obtain the code.

12. **(A)** Here,

    $$\text{SILVER} \to \text{SIL/VER} \xrightarrow{\text{Reversing}} \text{LIS/REV} \xrightarrow{+1} \text{MJT/SFW}$$

13. **(C)**
    Groan, Grotesque, Group, Guarantee.

14. **(B)**
    Nature, Nautical, Naval, Necessary.

15. **(B)**
    Foetus, Foliage, Foment, Forceps.

16. **(C)**
    Groan, Grotesque, Group, Guarantee.

17. **(B)**
    Nature, Nautical, Naval, Necessary.

18. **(B)**
    Foetus, Foliage, Foment, Forceps.

19. **(B)**
    Sun rises in the East. So, in morning, the shadow falls towards the West. Now, Mohan's shadow falls to his right. So, he is standing, facing south.

20. **(D)**
    In diagram (A) the directions are shown as they actually are. Diagram (B) is as per the given data. So, comparing the direction of North in (A) with that in (B), North will be called North West.

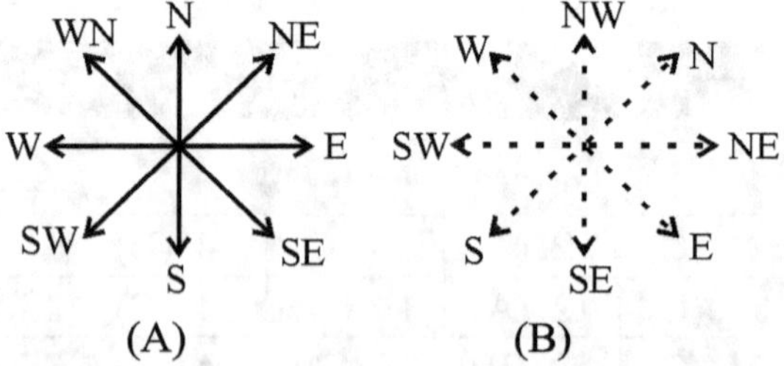

21. **(C)**

As per the given data, C faces towards West. D is to the right of C. So, D is facing towards South. Thus, B who is the partner of D will face towards North.

22. (D)

Knowledge is gained through experience or study, so learning is the essential element. A school (choice a) is not necessary for knowledge to take place, nor is a teacher or a textbook (choices b and c).

23. (D)

A culture is the behaviour pattern of a particular population, so customs are the essential element. A culture may or may not be civil or educated (choices a and b). A culture may be an agricultural society (choice c), but this is not the essential element.

24. (C)

An antique is something that belongs to, or was made in, an earlier period. It may or may not be a rarity (choice a), and it cannot be an artifact, an object produced or shaped by human craft (choice b). An antique is old but does not have to be prehistoric (choice d).

25. (D)

From figure I $(2 \times 2 - 1) = 3$
and from figure II $(5 \times 4 - 5) = 15$
From figure III $(5 \times 5 - 3) = 22$

26. (C)

For first triangle,
$10 - 4 = 6$
$18 - 10 = 8$
$18 - 4 = 14$
For second triangle,
$14 - 8 = 6$

$22 - 14 = 8$
$22 - 8 = 14$
For third triangle,
$11 - 5 = 6$
$15 - 11 = 4$
$\therefore ? = 15 - 5 = 10$

27. (C)

From figure I $(4 + 8) \times 9 = 108$
$\therefore ? = (5 + 4) \times 12 = 108$

28. (A)

Let the present ages of Sameer and Anand be $5x$ years and $4x$ years respectively.

Then, $\dfrac{5x + 3}{4x + 3} = \dfrac{11}{9}$

$\Rightarrow 9(5x + 3) = 11(4x + 3)$
$\Rightarrow 45x + 27 = 44x + 33$
$\Rightarrow 45x - 44x = 33 - 27$
$\Rightarrow x = 6$
$\therefore$ Anand's present age $= 4x = 4 \times 6 = 24$ years.

29. (D)

Let C's age be x years. Then, B's age $= 2x$ years. A's age $= (2x + 2)$ years.
$\therefore (2x + 2) + 2x + x = 27$
$\Rightarrow 5x = 25$
$\Rightarrow x = 5$
Hence, B's age $= 2x = 2 \times 5 = 10$ years.

30. (A)

Let the son's present age be x years. Then,
$(38 - x) = x$
$\Rightarrow 2x = 38$
$\Rightarrow x = 19$
$\therefore$ Son's age 5 years back $= (19 - 5)$
$= 14$ years

MODEL TEST PAPER

Answer Key

1. (C)	2. (B)	3. (C)	4. (C)	5. (B)	6. (B)	7. (C)	8. (C)	9. (D)	10. (B)
11. (B)	12. (B)	13. (A)	14. (B)	15. (D)	16. (C)	17. (A)	18. (C)	19. (B)	20. (A)
21. (B)	22. (A)	23. (D)	24. (B)	25. (C)	26. (D)	27. (D)	28. (B)	29. (C)	30. (C)
31. (B)	32. (A)	33. (A)	34. (B)	35. (A)	36. (B)	37. (D)	38. (D)	39. (D)	40. (C)
41. (C)	42. (D)	43. (C)	44. (A)	45. (B)	46. (A)	47. (B)	48. (B)	49. (A)	50. (C)

SAMPLE OMR ANSWER SHEET

1. STUDENT NAME (IN ENGLISH CAPITAL LETTERS ONLY)

Students must write and darken the respective circles completely using HB Pencil only. Othewise their Answer Sheets will not be evaluated.

PERSONAL DETAILS

2. SCHOOL CODE

3. CLASS

4. SECTION

5. ROLL NO.

6. QUESTION PAPER SET

A ◯
B ◯
C ◯
D ◯

7. MOBILE NUMBER

8. GENDER

MALE ◯
FEMALE ◯

9. STREAM
(Only for Class XI and XII Students)

MATHEMATICS ◯
BIOLOGY ◯
OTHERS ◯

MARK YOUR ANSWERS

	A B C D		A B C D
1.	Ⓐ Ⓑ Ⓒ Ⓓ	26.	Ⓐ Ⓑ Ⓒ Ⓓ
2.	Ⓐ Ⓑ Ⓒ Ⓓ	27.	Ⓐ Ⓑ Ⓒ Ⓓ
3.	Ⓐ Ⓑ Ⓒ Ⓓ	28.	Ⓐ Ⓑ Ⓒ Ⓓ
4.	Ⓐ Ⓑ Ⓒ Ⓓ	29.	Ⓐ Ⓑ Ⓒ Ⓓ
5.	Ⓐ Ⓑ Ⓒ Ⓓ	30.	Ⓐ Ⓑ Ⓒ Ⓓ
6.	Ⓐ Ⓑ Ⓒ Ⓓ	31.	Ⓐ Ⓑ Ⓒ Ⓓ
7.	Ⓐ Ⓑ Ⓒ Ⓓ	32.	Ⓐ Ⓑ Ⓒ Ⓓ
8.	Ⓐ Ⓑ Ⓒ Ⓓ	33.	Ⓐ Ⓑ Ⓒ Ⓓ
9.	Ⓐ Ⓑ Ⓒ Ⓓ	34.	Ⓐ Ⓑ Ⓒ Ⓓ
10.	Ⓐ Ⓑ Ⓒ Ⓓ	35.	Ⓐ Ⓑ Ⓒ Ⓓ
11.	Ⓐ Ⓑ Ⓒ Ⓓ	36.	Ⓐ Ⓑ Ⓒ Ⓓ
12.	Ⓐ Ⓑ Ⓒ Ⓓ	37.	Ⓐ Ⓑ Ⓒ Ⓓ
13.	Ⓐ Ⓑ Ⓒ Ⓓ	38.	Ⓐ Ⓑ Ⓒ Ⓓ
14.	Ⓐ Ⓑ Ⓒ Ⓓ	39.	Ⓐ Ⓑ Ⓒ Ⓓ
15.	Ⓐ Ⓑ Ⓒ Ⓓ	40.	Ⓐ Ⓑ Ⓒ Ⓓ
16.	Ⓐ Ⓑ Ⓒ Ⓓ	41.	Ⓐ Ⓑ Ⓒ Ⓓ
17.	Ⓐ Ⓑ Ⓒ Ⓓ	42.	Ⓐ Ⓑ Ⓒ Ⓓ
18.	Ⓐ Ⓑ Ⓒ Ⓓ	43.	Ⓐ Ⓑ Ⓒ Ⓓ
19.	Ⓐ Ⓑ Ⓒ Ⓓ	44.	Ⓐ Ⓑ Ⓒ Ⓓ
20.	Ⓐ Ⓑ Ⓒ Ⓓ	45.	Ⓐ Ⓑ Ⓒ Ⓓ
21.	Ⓐ Ⓑ Ⓒ Ⓓ	46.	Ⓐ Ⓑ Ⓒ Ⓓ
22.	Ⓐ Ⓑ Ⓒ Ⓓ	47.	Ⓐ Ⓑ Ⓒ Ⓓ
23.	Ⓐ Ⓑ Ⓒ Ⓓ	48.	Ⓐ Ⓑ Ⓒ Ⓓ
24.	Ⓐ Ⓑ Ⓒ Ⓓ	49.	Ⓐ Ⓑ Ⓒ Ⓓ
25.	Ⓐ Ⓑ Ⓒ Ⓓ	50.	Ⓐ Ⓑ Ⓒ Ⓓ

Signature of the Student & Date of Examination

Signature of the Invigilator & Date of Examination

www.ingramcontent.com/pod-product-compliance
Lightning Source LLC
LaVergne TN
LVHW060356200726
843506LV00003B/235